GIRAUDOUX:

LA GUERRE DE TROIE N'AURA PAS LIEU

by

ROY LEWIS
Lecturer in French,
University College of Swansea

EDWARD ARNOLD

© ROY LEWIS 1971

First published 1971
by Edward Arnold (Publishers) Ltd.
25 Hill Street, London W1X 8LL
Reprinted 1973

Cloth edition ISBN: 0 7131 5522 1

Paper edition ISBN: 0 7131 5528 0

Printed in Great Britain by
The Camelot Press Ltd, London and Southampton

Contents

JEAN GIRAUDOUX	6
1. INTRODUCTION	7
2. THE USE OF MYTH	13
3. THE PRESENTATION OF THE THEME	21
4. CASSANDRA	26
5. HECTOR	32
6. THE SUBLIME AND THE GROTESQUE	37
7. HELEN	42
8. ULYSSES	48
9. CONCLUSION	58
BIBLIOGRAPHICAL NOTE	63

Acknowledgements

We are grateful to M. Jean-Pierre Giraudoux for permission to use copyright material from *La guerre de Troie n'aura pas lieu* by Jean Giraudoux. Acknowledgement is also due for extracts from the following: *L'Ecole des Indifférents, Simon le Pathétique, Adorable Clio, La Française et la France* and *Introduction à la Charte d'Athènes*, by Jean Giraudoux (Grasset); *The Iliad*, translated by E. V. Rieu (Penguin Classics); *Helen of Troy* by John Pollard (Robert Hale); *The Ulysses Theme* by W. B. Stanford (Blackwell).

Jean Giraudoux

Jean Giraudoux (1882–1944) was born and brought up in provincial France, graduated with distinction from the Ecole Normale Supérieure in Paris, studied in Germany and America, and entered the French diplomatic service shortly before the First World War. His first collection of short stories, *Provinciales*, appeared in 1909. Returning to civilian life with a distinguished war record, he was responsible for developing French cultural services abroad and was in due course appointed Inspector of Diplomatic and Consular Posts, in which capacity he travelled widely. His meeting with Louis Jouvet in 1928 turned his attention to the theatre, and the success of *Siegfried* in that year inaugurated a series of plays which have caused him to be remembered primarily as a dramatist, although he continued to write novels until the end of his life. In 1939 he was appointed Minister of Information and entrusted, like Hector in *La guerre de Troie n'aura pas lieu*, with the task of averting a holocaust which could no longer be averted. He retired from public life after the collapse of France, refusing to co-operate with the occupying powers, and died in Paris in 1944 a few months before the liberation of the city.

His literary work was characterized by a highly imaginative, often humoristic, style, and revealed an original vision of the world. In addition to the plays, short stories and novels which form the major part of his literary output, he published imaginative impressions of his wartime experiences, literary criticism and a variety of essays on topics related to the state of France in his day. He also wrote the scripts of two films.

1. Introduction

The Trojan War did take place.

It happened some three thousand years ago, when the warrior kings of the Aegean banded together to sack the walled city which overlooked the Hellespont, or Dardanelles, the narrow strip of water linking Europe with Asia, the world of the Mediterranean with that which opens on to the Black Sea. They were seafarers and the route to the north was important to their trade. The war was but one incident in the long conflict of peoples and civilizations which characterized the area. We may wonder, in view of the later tales which came to be told about it, whether there were also dynastic issues involved in which some original of Helen of Troy played a part. All that we know with a reasonable degree of certainty is that after a long siege the city was taken and burned.

Just as this part of the world was one of the cradles of civilization, so by the same token it was one of the cradles of war. The Dardanelles have retained their strategic importance even into our present century. One of the bloodiest conflicts of the 1914–18 war resulted from an unsuccessful attempt by British and French troops to capture them from the Turks. Among those who took part in the campaign, being wounded and decorated for bravery in action, was Jean Giraudoux, then near the beginning of his literary career. He first saw the plains of Troy as a soldier.

The experience of the First World War deeply marked his subsequent writing. But it was not until twenty years after the disastrous Dardanelles campaign that he took the Troy story as the theme of what is perhaps his best-known play, *La guerre de Troie n'aura pas lieu*. When, in 1935, this paradoxical title appeared on the theatrical posters of Paris, the world was already sliding into another major conflict, and four years later the Second World War broke out.

We cannot say that Giraudoux came to his theme through his personal memories of war. It was in the pages of Homer that he first made the acquaintance of the characters whom he was to recreate on the stage. As early as 1911, in a collection of short stories entitled *l'Ecole des Indifférents*, he had touched in passing on the Trojan War in terms which strikingly anticipate the play which he was to write a quarter of a century later.

Il prétendait que le Destin de l'homme n'est que le hasard, que celui de la femme est une inéluctable logique. [. . .] Il essaya d'imaginer une femme vraiment libre, il tenta de diriger les héroïnes de l'histoire ou de la légende vers une existence de médiocrité ou de repos. En vain. Il ne pouvait, dans son imagination même, arriver à déplacer d'une ligne leur destin. [. . .] Il voulut empêcher la guerre de Troie.

He goes on to imagine a Menelaus who decides not to avenge the abduction of Helen. But in spite of his pacific intentions 'Troie devait périr', and the war takes place. The gossamer lightness of treatment of this early excursion into the realms of imagination is far removed from both the substance and tone of *La guerre de Troie n'aura pas lieu*, but the general outline of the play is already sketched in.

Among the factors which modified Giraudoux's treatment of his theme when he came to write the play must be included the fact that, in 1935, the threat of a Second World War was becoming very real. Giraudoux was by profession a diplomat, and well informed on the course which events were taking in the world around him. Moreover, he had identified himself particularly with the cause of peace between France and Germany, which he frequently stated was the most pressing problem of his age. He knew and loved both countries, and the possibility of reconciling the different concepts of civilization which they traditionally represented had been the theme of his first play, *Siegfried*, which was staged in 1928 to the accompaniment of protests from some of the more chauvinistic of his fellow-countrymen. When in 1935 he chose to re-examine the mythological presentation of events of pre-history, he must have seen some relevance between them and those of modern Europe. For his theme was not war itself but efforts to avert a war; and nothing could have been more topical at the time at which he wrote. But in fact the relationship of the play to its own time is neither obvious nor simple.

During the two or three decades that embraced the Second World War there was a strong feeling among intellectuals that an important writer owed it to them to have a 'message' of direct contemporary significance to communicate. As a result, works such as Anouilh's *Antigone* and Camus' *La Peste* were endowed with a political sense which is, to say the least, questionable. This feeling has been very apparent in judgments on *La guerre de Troie n'aura pas lieu*. Some critics have extolled the play as a trenchant comment on contemporary affairs. Others, finding it inadequate from this point of view, have played down Giraudoux's importance as a writer.

The desire to give the play contemporary significance has led to its being treated more or less as a political allegory. The confrontation of Greece and Troy, we are told, parallels that of France and Germany. Hector is to be regarded as the spokesman for Giraudoux's pacifist views. Against him are aligned the forces that make for war: Demokos the jingoist poet, playing on the irrational passions of the citizens of Troy; the self-seeking, heartless Helen; the unscrupulous Ulysses, and so on. It has never been made very clear what the function of such an allegory was supposed to be. Why should Giraudoux wish to suggest to the France of 1935 that all the efforts of its peacemakers would be in vain—without even recommending an alternative course of action?

The most one can say with certainty is that in 1935 the fact that war and peace were burning issues must have given the play a certain topicality. The obscurity of Giraudoux's 'message' did not worry his public, since the play was highly successful and ran for 274 performances; and the press comment of the time showed little awareness of its topic-ality. When it was revealed that the scene in which the international jurist, Busiris, appears had been omitted from the original production because—it was suggested—its irony might have an unhelpful effect on public opinion at a time when delicate negotiations were in progress, nobody seemed to mind very much. Any political implications the play might have appeared to be of secondary interest.

There are undoubted allusions to twentieth-century life in *La guerre de Troie n'aura pas lieu*. But this is not evidence that Giraudoux had in mind the events of his own time, since anachronism of this kind is a common feature of his style. It abounds in his early satire of Homeric material, *Elpénor*. In *Amphitryon 38* characters from Greek mythology indulge in trench warfare and live in houses with sash windows: in *Electre* they smoke cigars, while in *Judith*, set in Old Testament times, there are bankers and concert halls. Only a year before the appearance of *La guerre de Troie n'aura pas lieu* Giraudoux had published, in 1934, his novel *Combat avec l'ange*, the setting of which is French Government circles of the time, with the war-scares of the mid-thirties serving as back-ground to the action; but no one has ever suggested that this is in any sense a political novel. Further, despite the worsening international situation, the plays which Giraudoux wrote after *La guerre de Troie n'aura pas lieu* do not show any preoccupation with the political situation, and he was much criticized by advocates of *littérature engagée* because his contribution to the theatre in 1939, on the very eve of the catastrophe, was *Ondine*, an adaptation of the well-known (and decidedly non-political) tale by La Motte Fouqué.

This does not mean that Giraudoux had nothing to say about the events of his time, but rather that he did not treat them in the form of simple allegory, nor did he use the theatre as a political platform. He himself repeatedly declared that he did not mix his twin careers of diplomat and dramatist. In this respect his first play, *Siegfried*, is exceptional. When it was produced in 1928 its author gave several press interviews in which he stressed its contemporary relevance, and indeed spoke of it at times almost as a dramatization of a political pamphlet. And of all his plays, this is the one which has least successfully stood the test of time: it belongs to its own epoch rather than ours, and few save students of Giraudoux would bother to read it today. Seven years later, when speaking of *La guerre de Troie n'aura pas lieu*, Giraudoux showed a much wider concept of his subject. Asked by the correspondent of *Le Figaro* (21 November 1935): 'Faites-vous, dans votre pièce, des allusions aux événements d'aujourd'hui?' he replied: 'Aucune allusion, mais il est question de guerre et de paix.' He made no further reference to the topicality of the play on this or any other occasion.

There are many good reasons why Giraudoux may have wished to discourage any interpretation of his play which linked it too closely with his own time. In his lectures on the state of France in the 1930s, Giraudoux never refers to the threat of war with Germany. The fact that he held a diplomatic post and would therefore not be entirely free to speak his own mind may, in part, explain this; but in fact, Giraudoux adopts a positive and consistent approach to his material which makes such a hypothesis superfluous. Many French politicians and a large section of the public pinned their hopes for the future on the economic strangulation of Germany, the construction of impregnable concrete fortifications, and the suppression of all internal efforts to change the political and economic life of France. Giraudoux considered this approach vain and dangerous; and its main prop was appeal to popular fear of German aggression. The danger of German aggression came, in Giraudoux's view, not from Hitler's strength but from France's weakness. He saw his own country divided socially, paralysed by corruption and cynicism, and appallingly backward in every aspect of her economy. France had not moved into the twentieth century, and was incapable of summoning up either the will to survive or the economic resources to enable her to do so. Giraudoux's view was a realistic one. In 1939, France constituted a vacuum in the political life of Europe. It is doubtful whether Hitler's war of aggression would have been launched when it was if France had been united, conscious of her role in the world and able to fulfil it through the use of modern techniques. It is true that the capitulation of 1940 was due to the weakness of France rather than the strength of Germany. And it is also true to say that in the years which preceded the war, when Giraudoux approached a political subject he kept silent on the military threat but spoke with vigour on the state of France herself.

We should therefore not be surprised if *La guerre de Troie n'aura pas lieu* makes no attempt to analyse the nature of the threat to peace in 1935. It begs all the important questions which would preoccupy the historian. It deals with efforts to avoid a perfectly useless war. Thus it does not anticipate the Second World War, which was not useless but was fought for reasons which seemed then, and still seem to us, to be important; and which was brought about by circumstances in which the chauvinistic arrogance pilloried in certain parts of the play was not of decisive importance, at least on the French side.

In an earlier press interview, given to the correspondent of the *Echo de Paris* (6 November 1935), Giraudoux stressed that his re-use of classical material had more general implications than any considered above.

La guerre de Troie n'aura pas lieu est une comédie-tragédie. Vous y retrouverez tous les personnages de l'histoire: Hélène, Ulysse, Andromaque, Pâris. . . . C'est la guerre telle qu'elle se prépare.
— Est-ce une satire?
— Non, me répondit-il [. . . .] c'est une constatation.
Je pensai au film de Korda, *Hélène de Troie*, et à une transposition.
— Non—il avait deviné ma demande—ça ne prétend nullement être moderne . . . C'est l'heure qui précède une déclaration de guerre, l'effort que font ceux qui veulent l'éviter contre ceux qui la jugent inévitable, c'est tout le problème de ma pièce.

There is no reason for taking an author's view of his own work un-critically, since what he produces may not in fact be what he intended to produce. But his view should always be taken seriously. And the points which strike us in the statement quoted above are threefold:

Firstly, the play is not modern.

Secondly, it is not satirical in intent. From this it follows that characters such as Demokos—who is often regarded as being Hector's main opponent—are not central to the theme. It will be noted that Giraudoux does not, in fact, think him worthy of mention alongside the characters whom he has named.

Thirdly, the conflict is not between those who want war and those who want peace. All the main characters, in the final analysis, want peace: thus Paris joins with Hector (II xi, xii) as do Helen (II x, xi) and Ulysses (II xiii). The conflict is between those who believe that war can be avoided by an act of will followed by appropriate action and those who, for one reason or another, believe it cannot be avoided. The play is concerned with the limits of human freedom, and the question of the degree to which human intentions can modify the outcome of events.

Of course, we should not ignore Demokos, who is certainly satirized and unquestionably wants war. He is a caricature rather than a character, and all the protagonists of any real stature, whether Greek or Trojan, regard him with undisguised contempt. He is the means through which war is unleashed. But without the disastrous intervention of chance he would have been powerless. When Hector strikes him down, he still has time left to gasp out his false accusation that it is the Greeks who have murdered him. Had the javelin killed him instantly, there would have been no war—or, to be more exact, Destiny or chance would have had to bring it about by other means.

Giraudoux's concept of Destiny disconcerts us precisely because it shows the apparently trivial as having a more decisive influence on the course of events than any human intentions, however noble. André Gide saw this point clearly, and this was why he disliked *La guerre de Troie n'aura pas lieu*. He wrote shortly after Giraudoux's death:

> Non certes qu'il ignore la guerre et garde les yeux fermés sur les désolations qu'elle entraîne: mais encore dans les œuvres où elle intervient, dans celle dont elle est le sujet même, il travaille à la décontenance de toute signification raisonnable, de tout sens, entraîn-ant jusqu'au paradoxe une pensée trop encline au jeu . . . (Tombeau de Jean Giraudoux, in *l'Arche*, March 1944)

We need not accept Gide's criticism—for this aspect of Giraudoux's work is not merely negative, as Gide imagined—but we must take it into account in so far as it draws attention to a truth which is underestimated in all attempts to interpret the play as a political allegory. Giraudoux himself believed in the moral rightness of Hector's stand for peace. He demonstrated this in 1939 when, on the outbreak of hostilities, he accepted the post of Minister of Information in the vain hope that the catastrophe might yet be averted. Four years previously he had anticipated his own failure in *La guerre de Troie n'aura pas lieu*. He could not have wished to convince his audience of the vanity of such efforts. Nor is his play designed to spur the public on to greater efforts towards peace, for the stress on Destiny and chance nullifies any such interpretation, and the play does not leave in the public mind any clear picture of the course of action which Giraudoux is advocating. Thus the question of why he treats the theme in terms such as to provoke Gide's criticism must be given serious attention.

2. *The Use of Myth*

The narrator of one of Giraudoux's early novels, *Simon le Pathétique*, shares with his author the capacity to blend the present with the classical past. He interprets the world around him in terms of 'la fantaisie qu'exigent les humanités', and, travelling through Europe, describes himself as 'le voyageur qui baissait encore un peu la tête—un voyageur de grande taille—en entrant dans le port de Rhodes, pour ne point se heurter au colosse'. Mythology becomes for him an additional dimension of existence, and for this he pays tribute to his teachers:

> Je leur devais une vie large, une âme sans bornes. Je leur devais, en voyant un bossu, de penser à Thersite, une vieille ridée, à Hécube; je connaissais trop de héros pour qu'il y eût pour moi autres choses que des beautés et des laideurs héroïques.

La guerre de Troie n'aura pas lieu is the work of a more mature writer than the young author of *Simon le Pathétique*. Between 1913, when the novel was written, and 1935, the date of the play, there lies the First World War and the beginning of the collapse of an over-confident civilization. The mood of *La guerre de Troie n'aura pas lieu* is predominantly anti-heroic. But the youthful vision has not been extinguished. The characters of classical mythology are still, for Giraudoux, contemporaries.

These two factors—an intimate familiarity with certain aspects of the mythological past (for Giraudoux was an excellent classical scholar) and a repulsion from the grandiose ideals which had cost humanity so dear—go far to explain Giraudoux's approach to his subject.

That a dramatist should make use of a traditional theme, and that in the case of a French dramatist this theme should be taken from Greek mythology, need cause no surprise. In the golden age of French tragedy such themes were stock material, and the educational system ensured that every literate Frenchman had some acquaintance with the sources from which they came. Unlike the novelist, the dramatist is under no obligation to create his own characters and plot. The use of such material has not been entirely confined to the tragic theatre, but is particularly characteristic of it. The tragedian seeks to establish a certain distance between the scenes he represents and the audience's own time, in order to bring out the universal significance of his work; and mythological characters enjoy a high degree of detachment from the trivia of daily life. While comedy may be no less universal in its implications, it tends to deal with contemporary life and to stress its trivial aspects at the expense of universal pretensions.

By reason of its literary pedigree, Giraudoux's theme possesses something of the grandeur of tragedy. But by reason of the very familiarity with which he treats his characters, the play borders on comedy. Racine's heroes are unaware of the minor obligations which form so large a part of the daily round of human existence. They do not eat or sleep or discuss the weather: if they so much as sit down it is a gesture of great psychological import; and not even the prospect of death itself leads them to introduce a superfluous syllable into their impeccable alexandrines. But in Giraudoux the royal family of Troy is very much a family, with all the shades of antipathy and frivolity which familiarity engenders. When the most vital decisions affecting the future of them all are being made, Paris reacts as might any son in our own time who has unwittingly provoked a domestic crisis:

> Cette tribu royale, dès qu'il est question d'Hélène, devient aussi-
> tôt un assemblage de belle-mère, de belles-soeurs et de beau-père
> digne de la meilleure bourgeoisie. Je ne connais pas d'emploi plus
> humiliant dans une famille nombreuse que le rôle du fils séducteur
> (I vi).

The effect is not merely one of burlesque resulting from the disproportion between the presence of the characters and what in contemporary jargon we should describe as their 'image'. If we think of Hector as a contemporary, he appears as a young man whose life is *disponible*. Within the necessary limits imposed by the conditions of human existence, he can make of it what he will. In practice he will be, like all of us, a mass of inconsistencies, of qualities and defects. It is only in history and in biographies that a man assumes a definite role and a clear-cut personality: these are interpretations and simplifications. Subsequent generations cannot know the man as he was, but only the myth or myths which have been created about him, and which replace him. Posterity may know more about him actually than did his contemporaries, but this is not at all the same thing as we mean when we speak of 'knowing' a person in real life, for this involves our own personal contact with an incomprehensible creature of flesh and blood. When the final curtain comes down on *La guerre de Troie n'aura pas lieu*, Cassandra cries: 'La parole est au poète grec!' and Hector and all the other characters are handed over to Homer to prepare them for eternity. From then on they will be not what they were but what Homer makes of them, fixed in a role from which they cannot deviate.

This was the point which was stressed by Giraudoux in his interview, to which we have already briefly referred, with the correspondent of the *Figaro*:

— Ma pièce *La guerre de Troie n'aura pas lieu*, nous dit M. Jean Giraudoux, est une comédie dramatique, ou une tragédie bourgeoise, avec cette particularité que tous les spectateurs, ou du moins presque tous, sauront d'avance comment l'histoire se termine et aussi que la plupart des personnages vont être tués dans peu de temps.

— Ces personnages, les présentez-vous tels que la légende les a transmis?

— Je les présente du point de vue de leur intimité. Du fait même qu'ils sont des êtres vivants, ils ont des réactions qui n'ont pu être consignées par l'épopée. Ils ont, toutefois, le 'squelette' fixe que leur a donné la tradition. Je les prends avant qu'ils soient entrés dans la légende, alors qu'ils sont encore 'inemployés', que personne n'a parlé d'eux, même pas Homère.

The prescience of the audience is a necessary element in our appreciation of the play. This factor has been used by a number of writers for the twentieth-century theatre—including on occasions Giraudoux himself—

as a source of humour, pathos or irony. Its use in *La guerre de Troie n'aura pas lieu* is more complex.

Giraudoux does not simply retell a traditional story, giving it a contemporary twist. He apparently contradicts that story. And to do this with mythological characters produces a deliberately paradoxical situation which affects the significance and the impact of the play.

Even though they be presented as contemporaries, mythological characters are timeless. They exist in the imagination in a more or less fixed form: they have a 'squelette' which gives them what we may describe as a quality of necessity. This quality does not imply or necessarily depend upon their having been written about by great authors, nor do they need the grandeur of antiquity. All that is required is that they shall have been absorbed into the imagination of a people or a civilization so completely as to appear to exist in their own right. Sherlock Holmes assumed mythological stature despite his author, who tried in vain to kill him off but was compelled by popular clamour to resurrect his own creation. He had passed out of his author's control and assumed an independent existence. Whether such figures—whom Helen in Giraudoux's play calls 'vedettes'—have real existence or not is unimportant. The death of Rudolf Valentino, prince of lovers, evoked in 1926 a world-wide hysteria that no real person could have produced: the man of flesh and blood had been replaced by a celluloid image fabricated in the film studios. For years after James Dean, the young actor who represented, inarticulately, the frustrations of a whole generation, killed himself in a car accident, the studios were deluged with letters from a public which could not accept that he was dead. More recently, the producers of popular television series whose characters have become to millions more real than reality have, on allowing one of these familiar images to die, found themselves reviled as murderers.

For a literate public, the characters about whom Giraudoux writes have accumulated over the centuries this same quality of necessity which, however much they be modified, makes it inconceivable that they should not exist or that they should be radically other than they are. The title *La guerre de Troie n'aura pas lieu* does not merely imply a change of temporal perspective such as any historical dramatist has a right to demand of us, placing us at a point before the war happened. This it does incidentally: but its impact derives from the fact that it is essentially a challenge to credulity. We know that the Trojan War took place. What right has this dramatist to tell us otherwise?

In the terms in which the paradox is presented in the opening scenes, Giraudoux is asking us to believe that Hector will not be the immortal defender of Troy but a kind-hearted bourgeois *père de famille* dedicated to 'une existence de médiocrité et de repos'. That Andromache is not the distraught and despairing exile that Racine has shown us, but a young woman with the happiness and fulfilment of motherhood before her, and the consolations of a tranquil married life. The title is a paradox because it denies the one event which was to give these characters their nature and the immortality which enables us to know them. And when Giraudoux uses this title as the opening line of his play, he makes the paradox explicit. For Andromache does not say, as realism would demand: 'La guerre grecque n'aura pas lieu.' To a Trojan woman the war that threatens is no more 'the Trojan War' than any other in which the city has engaged. It was so named only by the Greeks after it had become a fact. She is in effect saying: 'The war which we all know took place will not take place'. And the paradox is maintained throughout the play. On a dramatic level, we are almost convinced that the war will not happen. The curtain has begun to fall before the blow is struck which precipitates the disaster. This is, of course, extremely good theatre, but it has, and is intended to have, disturbing implications.

The paradoxical nature of the play is not a gratuitous perversity on the part of the author. It reflects the paradox of human existence, that we act as if we are free without knowing whether we are: that we assume human morality to have value without knowing whether it has: that we act, as we think, 'purposefully', without ever knowing the outcome of our actions. In order to concentrate on this theme, it was necessary for Giraudoux to minimize the strictly political implications of his play. He does not offer war and peace as effective alternatives, depending upon the adoption of an appropriate course of action. In fact, apart from Andromache's brief moment of optimism in the opening scene, none of the characters has any great faith in the possibility of lasting peace. Even Andromache herself soon recognizes that there will always be wars. Hector fights for peace throughout the play, but he does so unsupported by any real belief in his ultimate success.

> Tous m'ont cédé. Pâris m'a cédé, Priam m'a cédé, Hélène me cède. Et je sens qu'au contraire, dans chacune de ces victoires apparentes, j'ai perdu. (I ix)

There is nothing in the actual political circumstances to justify this

B

pessimism: on the contrary, he appears to be winning. Yet this feeling haunts him to the end:

> Je gagne chaque combat. Mais de chaque victoire, l'enjeu s'envole. (II xi)

Demokos' wildest absurdities have failed to prevent the handing over of Helen to Ulysses, and all who control the city's destiny are agreed that there shall not be war. Only the purest chance—Hector's failure to silence Demokos with one blow—unleashes the catastrophe. To alter the whole outcome of a play by a random event occurring within the last few seconds before the fall of the curtain would normally be unthinkable. Yet we accept it because the play itself exists within the wider context of the legend, which we have never been allowed to forget. Nothing can alter the fact which has given these mythological characters their existence, the Trojan War. Thus Giraudoux's contradiction of the myth presupposes our knowledge that it cannot be contradicted, and from this ironical inconsistency springs the dramatic tension of the play.

This tension affects our emotional response to each of the main characters. When Cassandra foretells the coming disaster, we know that she speaks true, for that is her traditional role. The name of Andromache, in the opening scene, forms an ironical commentary on her anticipation of lasting peace, for long before Giraudoux shows her gazing out over a sea on which the first Greek prow has yet to appear, we have known her as Racine's exile and Baudelaire's bedraggled swan. The dialogue of Hector and Andromache discussing the future of their unborn child gains poignancy from our knowledge that the child will never grow to manhood, but will be snatched from his mother's arms and hurled to his death from the battlements on which they stand, when Hector is dead and the city crumbling around the survivors. Hector the pacifist we know as the heroic defender of Troy: in his person we feel the inconsistency of which we have already discussed some of the intellectual implications. Helen we see on the stage as a beautiful and dignified young woman; and in spite of the triviality which others seek to attribute to her, we know her as the immortal Helen of Troy, the prototype of all *femmes fatales*, who can say, in Tennyson's words:

> Many drew swords and died. Wher're I came
> I brought calamity.

And Ulysses brings with him a three thousand year old reputation for wisdom and cunning which leaves us in no doubt as to the sinister import of his words: the confrontation between him and Hector is that between the man who loves his city and the man whose stratagem will destroy it. All these characters we can appreciate, as Giraudoux presents them, with only a minimal knowledge of their background: but if we are aware of the tension between them and their mythological *persona*, our emotional response is greatly heightened.

There is, of course, no written original version of the story of the Trojan War. Homer takes it for granted that his audience knew the story, and concentrates on one episode, the quarrel of Achilles and Agamemnon. Other episodes may be pieced together from later fragments and allusions. The result is not history, nor does it form a chronologically coherent whole. We cannot place the Greek embassy to Troy to negotiate the peaceful return of Helen exactly in the sequence of events which led to the city's downfall, but, whenever it is supposed to have occurred, it clearly represents the point of no return in the progress towards war. It is apparent in Homer that the Trojans were divided on whether or not Helen should be sent back; but the infatuation of the old men, so much stressed in Giraudoux's play, is no more than hinted at in the *Iliad* and in spite of her beauty they favour her return. Homer's Hector is a warrior, not a negotiator, but he already shows the qualities apparent in Giraudoux's play; not only does he realize that it would be disastrous to stake Troy's future on Helen, but he is shown as a generous and very human character. This is particularly interesting when we remember that it is only through the myths of the Greeks, his enemies, that we know him. It is not unusual for warrior peoples to praise the valour of their enemies once they are conquered, for in so doing they enhance their own achievement in overcoming them: but the tribute paid to Hector is far more than this. The tenderness and love which Hector and Andromache show for each other is most unexpected in a 'heroic' literature which exalted violence, arrogance and passion: and Andromache's lament for the dead Hector is one of the most moving passages of the *Iliad*:

Husband, you were too young to die and leave me widowed in our home. Your son, the boy that we unhappy parents brought into the world, is but a little baby. And I have no hope that he will grow into a man: Troy will come tumbling down before ever that can be. For you, her guardian, have perished, you that watched over her and kept her loyal wives and little babies safe. [. . .] But who will mourn you as I shall? Mine is the bitterest regret of all, because you did not die in bed and stretching out your arms to me give me some tender word that I might have treasured in my tears by night and day. (*Iliad*, Book XXIV)

Thus Giraudoux's portrayal of Hector and Andromache, anachronistic though it may seem, is faithful to his original.

An awareness of the horrors of war is by no means unknown in Greek literature. Professor Rieu, in the Introduction to his translation of the *Iliad* (Penguin Classics, 1950), from which the above quotation is taken, claims that 'the *Iliad* was written not to glorify war (though it admits its fascination) but to emphasize its tragic futility'. If so, Giraudoux has certainly made this tendency more explicit, and has modified his characters accordingly. The actions of Homer's Hector, no less than those of Achilles, are governed by a heroic conception of honour which he must pursue even at the cost of his city's destruction, his own death and the bereavement of Andromache. Nothing of this is left in *La guerre de Troie n'aura pas lieu*. Here the pursuit of honour is seen as a threat to peace (I x); it stirs up the most primitive emotions (II xii), and its arch-advocate is the repulsive Demokos. The treatment of the concept of honour by Giraudoux is more than satirical: it is burlesqued. Hector is no Cornelian hero torn between the demands of 'la gloire' and more humane instincts and obligations. In all his actions, he is on the side of commonsense as the twentieth century understands it. But he has loved war, and, as Andromache shrewdly guesses, still does so in spite of his better judgment (I iii). Thus he is still the Hector of antiquity. And it is typical of Giraudoux's handling of his characters that this dichotomy does not express itself as an inner tension, to be explored in psychological terms, but is projected on to the outer world in the form of an exterior conflict. All that is, temporarily, in doubt is Hector's role in that conflict. In spite of the complexity of forces brought to bear upon him, he retains the simplicity of a character of ancient myth. One may say much the same of all the classical characters whom Giraudoux makes his own. Even Giraudoux's creations, Demokos and Oiax, would be as much at home in the world of antiquity as our own, though that world's judgment of the values they represent might be different from ours.

The characters, then, exist on several levels. They are their mythological, eternal selves. They are individuals in a drama which is unfolding before our eyes. And they are the reflection of the ideals, the hopes and the foolishness of the audience of any period, whether it be 1935 or our own age. Giraudoux's first audiences saw in Hector the young soldier back from the war which was, they supposed, to end all war; Andromache they saw as a young woman in a world where women were beginning to assert themselves, determined to overthrow the prejudices and passions of the past. We today may see in them a young couple under the shadow of the hydrogen bomb, trying to awaken, in a largely indifferent world, a sense of truly human values. In Demokos and his cronies the survivors of the First World War saw an old and corrupt generation which had sacrificed millions of young lives on the field of battle in the name of empty ideals. There can be no doubt that this feeling, as widespread in the inter-war years as in those which followed the Second World War, goes far to explain Giraudoux's concept of the old men of Troy.

3. The Presentation of the Theme

A synopsis of *La guerre de Troie n'aura pas lieu* might run as follows:

ACT I. On a sunny, peaceful afternoon Troy awaits the coming of the Greek ambassador Ulysses, sent to demand the return of Helen, whom Paris has abducted. If he is rebuffed, war will ensue. King Priam and the old men of Troy dote on this beautiful foreigner who has come among them, and will not give her up. But the army, led by Priam's eldest son Hector, returning from a victorious campaign, wants only to resume its peacetime occupations and will not fight for Helen. So much is revealed in the opening dialogue between Andromache, Hector's wife, and Cassandra, his sister, and in the reunion which follows between Andromache and Hector. Andromache is pregnant: Hector is determined that his son shall grow up in a world at peace, and in council with his father and the elder citizens of Troy insists that Helen be sent back to Greece. Demokos the poet claims that to refuse to fight would be a sign of weakness and decadence and leads the call to arms. The love of Hector and Andromache is parodied in the impotent lust of the old men of Troy for Helen, and the council of State becomes a family squabble between youth and age, men and women, reason and unreason, hypocrisy and sincerity, and leads to no clear conclusion. The act reaches its climax with the appearance of Helen and her confrontation by Hector. She appears completely indifferent to the fate of Troy. The curtain falls on a derisory portrait of Peace which negates the optimism and human values implied in the opening scenes.

ACT II. Helen begins her seduction of Troilus, Paris's younger brother. This dawn of love in the young and innocent is followed, when Demokos appears, by a satire on hate in the old and corrupt. The play moves to the level of pure tragedy with Hector's address to the dead and the ceremony of the closing of the Gates of War. The ceremony changes nothing. Andromache now admits there will be war, but appeals to Helen to give it some human meaning by loving Paris. Helen is unmoved. The Greeks arrive, and the resultant situation of acute danger is transformed into erotic comedy. The gods intervene in person through their messenger Iris, but their attempt to introduce moral values serves only to demonstrate that they are as absurd as the humans. The final dialogue between Hector and Ulysses leads to the conclusion that war is imminent. Unexpectedly, Ulysses offers peace and war seems to have been averted. No less unexpectedly the killing of Demokos by Hector, in a desperate attempt to prevent him inflaming popular anger against the Greeks, has the opposite effect when, in dying, he accuses the Greeks of murdering him. The curtain, which had begun to fall as Ulysses departs with Helen, rises again, the Greeks are massacred and war breaks out. As the Gates of War swing open, we see Helen complete her conquest of Troilus.

This is the material used by Giraudoux to conjure up a kaleidoscope of emotions, ranging through tenderness, pathos, the sublime and the farcical. High passion is absent, and so is sentimentality. The prevailing tone is one of irony, suffused with compassion.

For the most part, the characters are those of classical myth, and apart from Helen, queen of Sparta, and Ulysses, the Greek ambassador sent to demand her return, they belong to the royal family of Troy: Priam the aged king, Hecuba his queen, their sons Hector, Paris and the adolescent Troilus, and daughters Cassandra and the child Polyxena. Andromache, of course, belongs to the family by marriage. To these classical figures Giraudoux has added a motley collection of clowns, representative of human follies—the old men of Troy, a ragbag of 'experts' led by the supreme intellectual, the rabble-rousing poet

Demokos, some highly-sexed seamen and a drunken Greek warrior. And, hanging around the fringes of the action, a few gods and goddesses, personally represented by Iris, and the bedraggled figure of Peace. Oiax, it may be mentioned, is not the familiar Greek hero Ajax, despite the etymological similarity of their names: Giraudoux invariably used the current French versions of well-known names, and in any case the Ajax of the *Iliad* did not die, as does Giraudoux's character, before the outbreak of the Trojan War.

The play derives unity from the clear assertion of human values implicit in the moments of farce as in those of pathos and tragedy. We are not neutral observers: we are emotionally involved with Hector and Andromache. And there is a no less persistent recurrence, in various guises, of the concept of 'le destin' in which, however obscurely to the intellect, the nonsensical elements play their part. There is at every moment conflict, and though the grounds may change, the issues involved remain essentially the same. It is a conflict not only between characters but between attitudes which endeavour to give significance to the universe.

This unity of theme is supported by a unity of form which maintains dramatic tension. Exceptionally among Giraudoux's major works, this play has the simplicity of structure of classical tragedy. The scene does not move from Troy, and the time the action takes to unfold before our eyes is roughly that which would be required in real life. Giraudoux has based his play on a single episode which receives only brief mention in the Greek epic material. He has, indeed, simplified it, for according to tradition the Greeks sent two envoys to negotiate the return of Helen. Of these, Giraudoux eliminates Menelaus and retains Ulysses. From the opening lines we anticipate his coming, and the play ends with his departure. The division into two acts corresponds to the rhythm of the play, with Helen bringing the first to its climax and Ulysses the second.

Giraudoux is classical, too, in the economy of his stage directions. He tells us nothing of the personal appearance of his characters, nothing of their gestures and tone of voice. But he establishes his scene succinctly and effectively. A single phrase—'Terrasse d'un rempart dominé par une terrasse et dominant d'autres remparts'—serves as a continuing and silent commentary on the dialogue of the first act, as do the Gates of War on that of the second. They tell us all we need to know about the city, its history and its end. Giraudoux does not need to compete with other art forms having at their disposal other resources (such as we see, for instance, in Flaubert's evocation of ancient Carthage or the recreation of history in the modern 'spectacular' film), but, accepting the limitations of the theatre, uses them to good effect. The décor of any production of this play is more likely to be conventional than realistic, for Giraudoux is not attempting to recreate a moment of history.

All the characters speak a language which is their author's own. Whether king or common seaman, their speech is rich in imagery and unexpected intellectual associations, witty, ironical or poetic. They speak Giraudoux's language as naturally as Racine's use the *style noble* and the classical alexandrine. Individual characters are distinguished not by mannerisms of speech but by conflicts which set one against the other.

The characters do not analyse or question their own motives or actions. They have no 'psychology' as the term is usually applied to fictional figures, and therefore no psychological development. They represent different, sometimes simple, sometimes complex attitudes to living: if the characters change, it is because some change in circumstances has brought into prominence a new aspect of the concept they incarnate. They are not static types. They are constantly being provoked into action by challenges from outside them. 'Action' generally takes the form of speech, for language is the medium in which they exist and engage in their conflicts. No giralducian character exists in isolation. He does not need the traditional confidant, for each calls up his opposite as necessarily as, in Giraudoux's writing, the idea summons up the image; and the dialogue implies a constant antithesis.

Giraudoux's plays are battles of ideas. But they are not discussions or arguments. They show us, rather, the clash of incompatible concepts. Between Giraudoux's characters the common level of reasoning is often absent. They speak a language in which rational differences are implicit, rarely explicit. We have a clash of symbols which provokes an imaginative and emotional response, but the movement of the play rarely leaves us time to explore their precise intellectual significance. Andromache does not understand what Cassandra is talking about in the opening scene, and we, the audience, are involved in this lack of comprehension: and a similar situation prevails when Hector meets Helen or Ulysses. Apart from the scenes of burlesque, which possess the one-sided quality of a Voltairean *conte*, each of the characters is valid in his own context: the drama and tragedy arise from the fact that the worlds which their essences presuppose are mutually contradictory. What Helen says makes sense, but only in a world in which the values for which Hector fights are meaningless.

Paul Morand, who knew Giraudoux as well as any man, says of him in his *Adieu à Giraudoux*: 'C'était l'esprit le plus admirablement lucide que j'aie jamais connu.' This stress on lucidity is interesting. The obscurity of Giraudoux's style, when it is obscure, is due not to confusion of thought but to an awareness of the need to extend the bounds of human sensibility by developing the non-rational functions of language. Apart from a few isolated fragments scattered here and there in his works, Giraudoux wrote no verse: yet the nature of his vision and the form of his expression have caused him to be generally spoken of as a poet. He described himself as the poet who most closely resembled a painter. Language is for him a rich source of images, frequently visual. Abstractions become symbols. Andromache sees Peace as a sunlit mother-of-pearl Troy, with a soldier stooping in the saddle to stroke a cat; Cassandra sees it as a grotesquely made-up woman aping a seductiveness she has long ago lost. It is Cassandra who gives us the sleeping tiger of Destiny, which she awakens before our eyes and brings padding into the city and up the steps of the palace. Helen sees the future in coloured images which she does not attempt to explain. The final debate between Hector and Ulysses opens with a weighing of symbols one against the other.

Giraudoux's setting is that of the classical world, and his terminology and allusions are in general faithful to this. But he allows himself—rather less here than in some of his plays—the occasional anachronism, sometimes to comic effect, as when Demokos goes through the motions of taking a snapshot (II iii), sometimes to link up past and present, as in Ulysses' oblique reference to political negotiations at Locarno or Geneva. The style makes no attempt to pastiche that of Greek classical drama: it is literary but modern. Only in Hector's address to the dead is there conscious use of rhetoric to dramatic effect. At this point Giraudoux wishes to move us profoundly, and the tone of the play rises to that of tragedy. This speech would not be out of place on the tragic stage of the ancient world. As in all good rhetoric, art conceals art, and the balance and cadence of the sentences achieve an effect of apparently spontaneous simplicity. Hector's speech is also true to the pattern of tragedy in that it takes for granted that death is the end of significant sentient existence and consciousness. We should not attempt, from this, to draw conclusions about Giraudoux's own religious belief, which he never specifically states in his works. Here it is a necessary feature of the drama and of the tragedy. Even Racine and Shakespeare find themselves obliged to avoid Christian themes, but this does not mean that they rejected the religion of their age. Hector speaks in the context of his time and within a dramatic convention, and his view remains a significant aspect of man's experience of the world. The question of whether the universe may have some eternal significance which eludes man's comprehension must remain, for the dramatist, an open one.

4. *Cassandra*

Cassandra's name has become proverbial in all cultures which have inherited the Greek classical tradition. When Andromache declares, as the curtain rises:

La guerre de Troie n'aura pas lieu, Cassandre

the mere addition of her name to the assertion which forms the play's title turns it into a challenge to destiny. Cursed by Apollo, whose love she rejected, Cassandra's eternal role is to prophesy woe, to be disbelieved, and to be proved correct. When the play is finished, and the myth continues its inevitable way, she will run through the streets as the Trojans drag the Wooden Horse within their walls, warning them of the consequences of their act. They will ignore her, and Troy will perish. She herself will be raped, carried off into slavery, and murdered with Agamemnon on his return home. She is the symbol of lucidity in the face of disaster which she is powerless to avert.

The title of the play is one of the 'phrases négatives' which, as Cassandra tells Andromache, do not interest Destiny. But it is also by implication an 'affirmation'—a declaration of faith in lasting peace—and this aspect of it is a provocation to Destiny. In the conversation which opens the play, commonsense would seem to be on Andromache's side, and the fact that Cassandra is able so easily to undermine her position is in part due to the aura that she brings with her from her mythological past. Giraudoux takes advantage of this when he uses her to introduce, at the very beginning of the play, the concept of 'le destin' as the destroyer of human happiness. She will be used similarly to announce Andromache's pregnancy, the arrival of Hector, and that of Helen (I vi), and, in the closing words of the play, the failure of the attempt to liberate the characters from the course of events narrated by Homer.

But in Giraudoux's play she is a very human figure. If she possesses supernatural powers, they are shown only in the scene in which she conjures up Peace at the request of Helen, who has heard that she is a sorceress (I x). To Hector she is merely a younger sister useful for running errands and carrying out orders (I ii, ix), and Paris, no less brotherly, is too familiar with her to have noticed the beauty which won the heart of the sun-god (I iv). Andromache, very conscious of her status as wife and mother-to-be, patronizes her spinster sister-in-law: 'Le destin s'agite dans les filles qui n'ont pas de mari!' She is the prophetess without honour in her own family. Having endowed Helen with the gift of clairvoyance, Giraudoux did not wish to give her a competitor in Cassandra; her divination involves a typically giralducian combination of lucidity and instinct.

> Moi, je ne vois rien, coloré ou terne. Mais chaque être pèse sur moi par son approche même. A l'angoisse de mes veines, je sens son destin. (I x)

The quality of anguish distinguishes her from the other characters, and, if she had been given a more prominent part in the action, could have made of her a truly tragic figure. But La guerre de Troie n'aura pas lieu is not a tragedy in the traditional sense of the term, and Cassandra's role is restricted, though important. It is appropriate that we should be first introduced to the concept of Destiny through one who knows that she has no influence on the course of events, while being at the same time deeply aware of her own involvement in them. When Helen and Ulysses speak of Destiny, they speak as foreigners, and we may be tempted to interpret their words as motivated by self-interest. But Cassandra belongs to a doomed family and a doomed city. Her role is that of victim.

The stress on feeling serves to differentiate her strongly from Helen, to whom the words quoted above are addressed. They imply a capacity to respond intuitively to the essential nature of things, and thus to know what these things have it in them to become. But in her confrontation with Andromache which opens the play she expresses her awareness in terms of more general applicability which serve to prepare us for the action which is to follow.

> Je ne vois rien, Andromaque. Je ne prévois rien. Je tiens seulement compte de deux bêtises, celle des hommes et celle des éléments.

The play will explore these two concepts side by side, and interrelate them.

Both Cassandra and Andromache display a combination of instinct and reasoning which we commonly consider as essentially feminine—possibly because in women the one masks the other less effectively than in men. Andromache's view of the world in the opening scene is the result of her love for Hector and her unborn child, but later (II viii) she is to show an awareness of the situation as realistic as that of Ulysses. In the first scene, the barrier of incomprehension which separates the two women who face each other on the battlements of Troy is absolute, and Andromache's allusion to Cassandra's virginity is to the point. Her own view is an essentially homocentric one, for she is ensnared in the web of personal relationships which visionaries and mystics traditionally eschew. Although Cassandra too is personally involved, her vision goes beyond personal considerations and is essentially cosmic. To Andromache the situation is simple enough. Helen and Paris no longer love each other, therefore Helen will return to Greece and there will not be war. It is a matter of commonsense. Cassandra does not have much faith in commonsense: to her the governing characteristic of the world is 'la bêtise'. She sees human absurdity as the corollary of the absurdity of the cosmos. One of the characters of Giraudoux's *Intermezzo* defines Humanity as having the object 'd'isoler l'homme de cette tourbe qu'est le Cosmos', and Hector, when he fights in *La guerre de Troie n'aura pas lieu* 'pour fabriquer une heure qui soit à nous' (I ix), sets himself the same aim. Cassandra seeks to place man in his cosmic setting by giving Andromache two definitions of Destiny.

In the first place, it is 'la forme accélérée du temps'. Andromache does not understand this abstract assertion, and, possibly, neither does the audience, though it arouses our curiosity and makes it clear to us that she is thinking in terms quite different from those which appear important to Hector's wife. So, with Cassandra, we go straight on to her second definition, the 'métaphore pour jeunes filles'. In a study such as this, we must necessarily examine the ideas in greater depth than is possible or desirable in the course of the actual theatrical experience, and we shall therefore return to this first definition, which any student of Giraudoux will recognize as being characteristic of his thought; for he often represents the fundamental discord between gods and men as being due to their existing in totally different scales of time. But it is appropriate to consider the second definition first, since this is the one which predominates in the theatre, and only in retrospect do we appreciate the importance of the first.

Cassandra's image of the tiger may seem to have little in common with 'la forme accélérée du temps' save the speed of the beast's final bound upon its prey. The metaphor is a visual development of the proverbial 'Ne réveillez pas le chat qui dort.' (In French it is sleeping cats, not sleeping dogs, that should be let lie.) Its impact is immediate, and it is developed with such dramatic force that Christopher Fry has used it as the title of his English translation of the play. We see Destiny as a force outside man which normally is harmless enough since he and it are indifferent to each other. But the sleeping tiger is awakened by 'des affirmations' (admirably translated by Mr. Fry as 'cocksure statements') which Cassandra contrasts with 'des phrases négatives' which do not disturb it.

Cocksure statements imply positive actions, and the action which is in process of awakening the tiger is the abduction of Helen by Paris. For Andromache, the importance of this act depends simply on its human significance—'Pâris ne tient plus à Hélène. Hélène ne tient plus à Pâris,' and therefore the episode is closed. But for Cassandra, every act produces consequences: what is done cannot be undone by denying its significance. She challenges Andromache's basic assumption that the significance of an act depends upon human values and human motivation. This act must be set in its context, which is that of the rise and fall of civilizations.

The supreme example of the cocksure statement is the claim that 'le monde et la direction du monde appartiennent aux hommes en général et aux Troyens ou Troyennes en particulier'. This belief is an example of 'la bêtise des hommes', but it is also, *mutatis mutandis*, a necessary corollary of civilization, which is built on this illusion. Every civilization represents a more or less successful attempt to impose human values on a primeval chaos. Necessarily, it believes that its own standards are 'right', and it is this self-assurance which gives it the force to establish itself. But when it is at its peak it tends to forget the primeval chaos and to become complacent, imagining the battle to be won: it assumes that its standards and values are natural and inevitable, that they are, in fact, those of the world itself. Then its doom is sealed. It replaces reality with a dream, and is no longer adapted to the needs of man on what Giraudoux describes, in *Juliette au Pays des Hommes*, as 'cette planète qui lui a été dévolue par hasard'.

Andromache, looking on her sunlit city, sees it as the culmination of a process leading to human happiness. The past is to be wiped out: there will be no more war: families will live in peace and develop their human qualities, because she feels instinctively that this is right. Doubtless it would be right in a world made for humans, but that is not the world Cassandra sees. It is left to Priam to point out to Andromache that she owes her very existence and the prosperity of her city to the fact that her ancestors were warriors (I vi). Time cannot be stopped at the point which suits our convenience, or the progress of history interfered with because we happen to like the present state of affairs.

The assertion that human values are paramount provokes Destiny. Our own age, seeing itself as the culmination of history, may believe that if only it can abolish the hydrogen bomb it will inaugurate an era of peace and humanity in which the world as a whole will learn to conform to our present-day ideals. Cassandra sees lying beyond us other civilizations waiting to be born from our ruins, or other barbarisms, or perhaps an eternity of nothingness. Our very idealism, no less than our chauvinism, she would see as a form of complacency, a form of arrogance, which will bring us into disastrous contact with the realities of the irrational, non-human world. Though vastly different in its moral significance, the generous vision of Hector and Andromache is no less a demonstration of 'la bêtise des hommes' than the stupidity of Demokos, and it is from the conflict of 'la bêtise des hommes' and 'la bêtise des éléments' that Destiny is made.

We are now in a position to re-examine Cassandra's original definition of Destiny as 'la forme accélérée du temps'. At its simplest level, this is a vision of history which embraces a wider sequence of events than comprehensible to the human mind in the time-scale of normal life. In *Ondine*, Giraudoux speaks of the dramatist as one who accelerates time. He takes events which, in the normal time-perspective, would be scattered apparently at random throughout a lifetime, and, by contracting them into the space of two hours, establishes a cause-and-effect relationship which could not be apparent to the characters themselves but which possesses, for the audience, the quality of inevitability. Applying this to Cassandra's definition, we may say that at the normal speed of time we cannot comprehend the plot of the play in which we are actors, though we are free to imagine illusory ones centred on ourselves. But the author of the play is really the Cosmos, or what we have, since Giraudoux's time, become accustomed to speak of as the 'absurd universe': absurd, that is, because it is indifferent to human values and incomprehensible to the human mind. We are at the mercy of 'la bêtise des éléments', small-part actors in a play we have not chosen and the ending of which is unknown to us.

If the speed of exposure of a motion picture camera is slowed down and the resultant film projected at normal speed, what we see is an acceleration of time. This can produce a hilarious transformation of the most ordinary events, as the directors of comedies in the days of the silent screen knew very well. If we increase the intervals between exposures not merely by a fraction of a second but by hours or even days, still more startling results can be obtained. We see the petals of a flower unfold before our eyes, and its growing stem writhe in the air like a serpent. And yet in our normal time-perspective we think of the flower as immobile. Had we but world enough and time, we could produce a motion picture which would show continents changing shape and drifting across the oceans, rivers twisting and turning like living things as they erode away their valleys, whole mountain ranges rising and falling. We could show human history as a flicker between two ice ages; life itself, perhaps, as an interlude in a sterile eternity.

That is our world. But it is not the world as we see it. The difference is one of temporal perspective. The limitations of our vision are necessary if we are to attribute paramount importance to human values. On a cosmic scale, of what importance is it whether Andromache's son lives or dies, whether peace prevails or Troy perishes? If, like Cassandra, we who are normally only vaguely aware of the universe as a force outside ourselves could see time in its accelerated form, we would be aware that we are involved in a cosmic process completely beyond our control. The stable world in which we think we live simply does not exist. We navigate a slow-moving river, scarcely aware of its current: Cassandra sees it as a raging torrent carrying us towards the rapids.

It is small wonder that she describes as 'épouvantable' a definition of Destiny which seems, at first glance, innocuous enough.

Cassandra's view may be described as a lucid pessimism. It does not imply the absolute fatalism of Helen's coloured visions, which destroys all motive for human action. Cassandra acts morally, though without much hope for the efficacity of her actions. She sides with Hector against Demokos, she identifies herself with human values against the absurdity which will ultimately prevail. As she herself stresses, she cannot foresee the future, but she knows that that future will take no account of human interests. She interprets the world with an acute sensibility; prevented by her lucidity from taking refuge in the illusions which make human life tolerable, she cannot, like Helen and Ulysses, dissociate herself from the coming catastrophe. Hence the anguish which she feels at the approach of any living thing, for its destiny, the product of the clash of 'la bêtise des hommes et la bêtise des éléments', is unlikely to be a happy one.

5. Hector

The hero of *La guerre de Troie n'aura pas lieu* is on the stage practically throughout the play, and he engages our sympathy from the beginning. We see him, as we see the other principal characters, through the eyes of others before he actually makes his appearance. The opening scenes in which Cassandra sets out her view of Destiny serve to effect this introduction. It is as husband, father to be, champion of peace and sole defence against Cassandra's sombre prognostications that Andromache presents him, and his appearance, followed by a scene of great tenderness, completely changes our perspective. Cassandra's cosmic view gives way to human values. Certainly Hector's entry is ill-omened. He comes in at the precise moment when Cassandra has led us, and a terrified Andromache, to expect the tiger to push open the door with its muzzle. In this we may see prefigured, not only his destiny as a warrior, but the fact that it is his javelin-thrust which will unleash disaster. But such forebodings are dissolved in the warmth of the love of this young couple. We are caught in the trap. Like her contemporaries we forget Cassandra and are ready to accept that they, and not her inhuman Destiny, represent the true values of the world.

A whole generation of war-sickened Frenchmen could see themselves in Hector. Like him they had gone to war thinking it noble and glorious. Like him they had returned disillusioned, convinced that if human values were to survive another war must be avoided at all cost. Like him they were adamant that the young, who had borne the brunt of battle, should be the ones to decide the future. And yet, accepting this fact, we find that the conversation that follows is not what we should expect. Andromache has been more convinced, if not by Cassandra's arguments, at least by her imagery, than she cared to admit to her face, and once Cassandra is off the stage she adopts her viewpoint. She does so in the hope that Hector will prove her wrong. But the most he can offer is the belief that this particular war will be averted because its potential cause is so frivolous and so easily put right. But there will always be war. Hector himself has loved war, and humanity will always love it. His own son will grow up to be a warrior.

The generation of the mid-twentieth century, at least in technologically advanced countries, will find this ambiguous attitude to war more than a little strange. Our technology has created a situation in which a stable society, affording the maximum happiness to everyone, appears theoretically possible. The major threat to its realization comes from war. And this same technology has changed the nature of war. To love saturation bombing or the horror of Nagasaki or the use of napalm on defenceless populations would be unthinkable save to the subhuman or the monstrous. And yet, unlike the literature of disillusionment which followed the two World Wars, unlike Shaw's *Arms and the Man* which dates from the end of the nineteenth century, Giraudoux's Hector accepts that man can love war. He does not put the blame for it on scheming or blundering politicians, nor on plutocrats and imperialists pursuing their own selfish interests at the cost of the helpless masses. He puts responsibility for war firmly on the shoulders of ordinary men like himself.

Hector is not a violent man. But he is a man of action. He wants to get things done, to put things right. And this attitude leads to violence. War for him has meant adventure and conquest and liberation from the dull routine of existence. It has meant comradeship with his fellows in danger, and the urge to pit his strength against others. These are characteristics of man, and particularly of youth. It remains to be seen (if we

c

are given the opportunity) whether they can find any outlet in a pro-longed period of peace. Perhaps they could if it were not for two other human characteristics of which Hector himself is innocent but which he meets in Demokos and his supporters—arrogance and hatred. In one of his last and most pessimistic plays, *Sodome et Gomorrhe*, Giraudoux defines war as 'le jour où l'âme humaine se donne à sa nature'. King Priam does not hate; but as figurehead of one of the great cities of the ancient world, a city whose wealth and grandeur owe their existence to the fighting instincts of its young people, he has no doubt that the significance of an individual life lies in its capacity for self-sacrifice to a cause greater than itself.

> Cette occupation terne et stupide qu'est la vie se justifie soudain et s'illumine par le mépris que les hommes ont d'elle. [. . .] Il n'y a pas deux façons de se rendre immortel ici-bas, c'est d'oublier qu'on est mortel. (I vi)

The generation of 1914, which saw in war a splendid and noble adventure, could well have understood these sentiments. Giraudoux himself had certainly understood them. Death in battle was a hazard he had faced willingly enough. Paul Morand tells us in his *Souvenirs de notre jeunesse* that on hearing of his intention to volunteer for active service Giraudoux wrote to him from the hospital where he was recovering from his wounds:

> Je serai bien attristé, mon cher Paul, de te savoir au feu, mais com-ment ne pas t'approuver? Tu verras d'ailleurs des choses si effrayantes et si fantastiques qu'on sacrifierait volontiers son bras droit pour les avoir vues. Tant pis aussi pour la vie! Tout serait si simple si nous n'avions pas de parents! Pour eux seuls la guerre est une calamité.

These were the words of a young man in his early thirties who, although he loved France deeply, also loved the Germany against which he was fighting. At the end of the conflict his emotions were simple enough: 'Ce que je suis? Je suis un vainqueur, le dimanche à midi'—a cry devoid of arrogance, full of the sense of an adventure brought to a successful conclusion, which victors of all ages in the past might have uttered but which would turn sour on modern lips. When, two years after the armistice, Giraudoux published his *Adorable Clio*, he prefixed to it an epigraph which is that of a lover addressing the loved one he is abandoning:

Pardonne-moi, ô guerre, de t'avoir—toutes les fois où je l'ai pu—caressée . . .

Giraudoux had loved war. But the affaire was over. Thirteen years later, when he wrote *La guerre de Troie n'aura pas lieu*, he no longer loved it.

In this, Hector reflects his author. He does not so much explain his conversion as express it—as all Giraudoux's characters express their attitudes—in terms of a relationship with the external world. He uses an image based on the sounds of war, assimilated imaginatively to a musical scale. The sounds of war had been tuned, as on a piano keyboard, to give a satisfying harmony. Now they produce a discord. They no longer 'ring true'. But he is also a little more specific than this.

Auparavant ceux que j'allais tuer me semblaient le contraire de moi-même. Cette fois j'étais agenouillé sur un miroir. Cette mort que j'allais donner, c'était un petit suicide. (I iii)

The psychologist would say that he has acquired a capacity for empathy. He can put himself in the position of other people. We might say that he has become adult. He has, in any case, lost that quality which elsewhere Giraudoux describes as 'innocence', the capacity simply to follow one's own nature, to be oneself regardless of all moral considerations, as uninhibited as any non-human creature. From now on he will put other people's interests before his own—a quite different thing, one may add, from the hypocrisy so common in public life of using the furthering of other people's interests as a pretext for asserting one's own ego. He can no longer accept that the zest of self-fulfilment which man knows in fighting can justify war. His life will be, like that of another of Giraudoux's characters, Jérôme Bardini, 'cette vie plus faite de la vie des autres que de la sienne propre'.

Hector never shared the meanness of Demokos. His revulsion against war is greatly intensified by his realization that the generous courage which leads young men to sacrifice their lives can be manipulated by the stupid and self-interested. Troy may have been built on war, but not on the vainglorious mouthings of chauvinistic hate. The city has changed, as Giraudoux's world seemed to have changed. Hector sees the coming war as unjust and futile, but he does not reject it merely for that reason. He rejects war itself. This is a moral choice. But in spite of himself, he remains a warrior. The javelin hurled to silence Demokos is a weapon used in the cause of peace, but it is still a weapon. Man will fight, even to maintain peace: and so there will be war.

All Hector's judgments are those of a man of action. He assesses each situation empirically. Apart from his overriding aim, which is to ensure for man the right to live in peace, he has no moral concepts. Although his cry to Busiris, 'Trouve une vérité qui nous sauve. . . . Forge-nous une vérité' (II v), is not as cynical as it sounds, given the imbecility of the international jurist to whom it is addressed, the fact remains that the only truth in which Hector would be remotely interested is one which preserves peace. He is perfectly ready to lie to Ulysses about the sexual relations between Paris and Helen if, in so doing, he can save Troy. He would be willing to kill Helen. In each demonstration of moral anarchism, the relationship between the characters is so managed that we sympathize with Hector. We accept this because, by his choice of subject, Giraudoux has seen to it that we know in advance that the alternative to his course of action is not just a war but a war of total annihilation. Human survival is a prerequisite of morality.

In this, Hector anticipates in its essentials his author's own stand on the outbreak of the Second World War. After writing and lecturing through the years in an attempt to purge the more corrupt elements of French life (and his works in this field, *Pleins Pouvoirs*, *Sans Pouvoirs*, *La Française et la France* and others, are still worth reading), he accepted office in 1939 in a government which in many respects represented that corruption, because to him the physical survival of France was of vital importance and took precedence, if the choice had to be made, over any ideal. His aim, unrealizable as we now know it to have been, was to prevent the stalemate of the 'phoney war', during which both sides glowered at each other from behind their concrete fortifications, from exploding into the cataclysm before which France was to crumble in the following year. And when collapse had become a fact, Giraudoux made it clear, in *Armistice à Bordeaux*, that he accepted capitulation however dishonourable it might be. There were many, he wrote, who believed that France should have resisted to the point of extinction in order to maintain her integrity. But more important than this, in Giraudoux's view, was that France should survive.

This was a practical decision taken *in extremis*. So too is Hector's. *La guerre de Troie n'aura pas lieu*, which deals with an absurd war, does not really pose the question of whether there may not be some moral principles for which life may be justly sacrificed. But two years later it was followed by *Electre,* in which the heroine allows her city to be destroyed rather than compromise on her concept of moral principle. The tone of this play is considerably different from that of *La guerre de Troie n'aura pas lieu.* It would be wrong therefore to regard Hector as being in any absolute sense the mouthpiece of Giraudoux. The dramatist sees further than Hector. He cannot make Hector succeed, but he can bring out the value of his stand.

Hector takes us from the cosmic vision of Cassandra to the field of ordinary human relationships. He is concerned not with the mindless universe but with man's love of his fellows and his love of war, and consequently with opposing desires and ideals which men may consider more important than human survival. He chooses peace, and it is not in the nature of the play to question his choice. In his struggle, Andromache stands at his side. If there is a danger that woman's purity be used as a pretext for war, then she will argue that woman is fundamentally corrupt (I vi). Priam realizes that she, no less than Hector at this point, is guilty of *mauvaise foi*; but in the context, when war may apparently still be averted, we feel that she is right in what she does. Later, when she has accepted that war is inevitable, she will change her position and beg Helen to love Paris so that the war may be given some semblance of human significance (II viii). Hector, on the other hand, stands firm. When he accepts war in the closing scenes of the play, it has no meaning for him, nor does he seek to give it any.

Within the limits of his knowledge and his circumstances Hector is, as Demokos derisively tells him, a 'realist'. The irony of the situation is that while we admire and respect and love him for his realism, he is, of all the characters, the one who understands least the course which events are taking around him.

6. *The Sublime and the Grotesque*

If Hector lacks all intuition of 'la bêtise des éléments', he nevertheless shows great dexterity in dealing with the more crudely anti-social manifestations of 'la bêtise des hommes'. The fact that Giraudoux does not face him with any serious (i.e. thought-provoking) political problems obviously facilitates his task in some respects. In real life, the diplomat is constantly called on to reconcile the irreconcilable, and the most he can hope for is to choose the lesser of two evils. Hector, on the other hand, is faced with simple black-and-white issues. There can clearly be no sense in fighting a war over Helen, and lest there should be any doubt in our minds about that, Giraudoux uses as representatives of the pro-war party characters who might well come straight out of an Astéryx comic strip. Figures such as Demokos, the Geometer, Busiris and Oiax have no mythological ethos to give them depth: they are simple caricatures invented by Giraudoux to burlesque the human absurd. And yet, in his contest with them, Hector loses.

This type of burlesque is characteristic of Giraudoux's writing from the very beginning. Boswell tells of a certain lawyer who remarked to Dr. Johnson: 'You are a philosopher, Dr. Johnson. I have tried too in my time to be a philosopher; but I don't know how, cheerfulness was always breaking in.' This was a man after Giraudoux's own heart. The intellectual, or philosophical, content of Giraudoux's work is pessimistic, but the material is treated as often as not on a level of ironical humour. For him, the capacity to laugh at the absurdity of the human condition was one of the strongest defences against the intellectual pessimism implied in Cassandra's view of the world. This is one reason why he has been more readily appreciated by other creative writers and by the general public than by scholars, who, being prone to regard works of art as quarries from which to extract ideas, are irritated by his apparent failure to take life seriously. But this attitude to living is important in Giraudoux. In considering the clowns of *La guerre de Troie n'aura pas lieu*, we must naturally analyse their significance to the intellect, but this should not distract attention from the fact that, in the theatre, we enjoy the element of clowning for its own sake.

But the first opponent Hector has to meet is neither grotesque nor foolish; and he has a respectable classical pedigree. This is his younger brother Paris. Following the very human love scene of Hector and Andromache, Paris presents us with another concept of love, which will give place in turn to a third concept, that of the lascivious and impotent old men of Troy. This series represents a progressive degeneration, a growing divorce between the real and the ideal. There is a necessary connexion, within the play, between the themes of love and war, since the destruction of Troy results from the abduction of Helen

by Paris. Andromache's initial assumption that Helen will return to
Greece is based on her intuitive awareness that they do not love each
other, at least as she understands the term in the light of her own experience. But love means different things to different people. The two
forms opposed to each other in *La guerre de Troie n'aura pas lieu* may
be described as realist and romantic.

Andromache accepts that marriage is a union, for better or for worse,
between imperfect humans. It involves coming to terms with another
person.

> On ne s'entend pas, dans l'amour. La vie de deux époux qui s'aiment,
> c'est une perte de sang-froid perpetuelle. La dot des vrais couples
> est la même que celle des couples faux: le désaccord originel. Hector
> est le contraire de moi. Il n'a aucun de mes goûts. Nous passons
> notre journée ou à nous vaincre l'un l'autre ou à nous sacrifier. Les
> époux amoureux n'ont pas le visage clair. (II viii)

Hecuba too has lost any illusions she may have had on human nature,
and on men in particular: she well realizes the inadequacy of her ageing
husband Priam, who dotes on Helen and leaves to his son Hector the
task of saving the city. But she is loyal to him, and allows herself no
other infidelity than to dream of the man he might have been, and
doubtless once was.

> *Priam:* Tu m'as trompé, toi?
> *Hécube:* Avec toi-même seulement, mais cent fois. (I vi)

This love and faithfulness between human beings spreads out to
embrace future generations: it has significance for mankind and holds
promise for the future. Contrasted with this, the Don Juanism of Paris
is isolated and sterile. For him, the woman does not exist as a person.
She is an image who evokes a feeling, and the feeling alone is important.
He cultivates that aspect of the sexual instinct which makes the unfamiliar
perpetually inviting, the familiar necessarily uninteresting. This is the
essence of Romanticism: not merely Byronic Romanticism, but Romanticism in all its forms. His light-hearted and witty commentary on love
is very different in tone, but not fundamentally in approach to its subject,
from the lamentations of a Lamartine or a Musset more easily moved
to eloquence by the loss of a loved one than by her presence. Hugo's
Tristesse d'Olympio is not a tribute to Juliette Drouet, but an aesthetic
substitute for her. The death of Leopoldine produced in Hugo a turbulence of spirit which was resolved in the creation of great verse, but the

existence of *A Villequier* does not imply that the poet was a good father or had any particular interest in his surviving daughters. Such considerations are irrelevant to an assessment of the aesthetic value of the poems, but relevant to an understanding of the nature of Romantic love. It is not without reason that Giraudoux permits Paris his anachronistic parody of Lamartine's 'Un seul être vous manque, et tout est dépeuplé' (I iv). Love, as Paris understands it, would be irreparably spoilt by the prolonged presence of a real woman.

This we may accept without too much indignation from Paris, for being young, handsome, rich, and having the most beautiful woman in the world at his disposal—one who, being a daughter of Jupiter, is perpetually 'distant'—we would scarcely expect him to be a model of responsibility. He has charm, and, in spite of his youthful egoism, is capable of acting seriously: he gives up Helen, if only to save his self-respect (I vi), and puts up with a good deal, in the face of Ulysses' sarcasm, to help his brother (II xii). But our reactions are very different to Demokos and the old men of Troy, who lack both his charm and his excuse. The master of French comedy, Molière, derives much of his humour from the spectacle of the hypocritical old going through the motions of a love which is natural and sympathetic in the young and generous-hearted. Giraudoux's comic method, in this case, is not dissimilar. What we find amusing in youth becomes grotesque in old age.

It may seem strange that Giraudoux, himself a poet and a Symbolist who had no taste for realism, should so savagely pillory poetry and Symbolism in the person of Demokos, and so obviously align himself with the realist Hector. True, Demokos is a bad poet, but he is the sole representative of poetry in the play, and Hector condemns poetry as such, not just bad poetry, as the sister of war (I vi). There can be little doubt that he, like Plato, would exile all poets from his republic, and in the context of the play we can hardly blame him. The fact that Demokos is dangerous does not derive from the quality of his verse, but had he been a good poet our attitude to him would have been complicated by factors irrelevant to the play. All satire involves a deliberate ignoring, or an inability to comprehend, qualities which may belong to the object attacked. What would have been left of Voltaire if he had acquired a capacity to understand metaphysical thought?

Giraudoux remarks, in *Simon le Pathétique*, that a young man may live on moral credit: we judge him on his potential. But an old man can only be judged on his life. Demokos, like those for whom he speaks, is empty and thoroughly corrupt. He conceals the inadequacies of reality behind a barrage of words. Incapable of love, he exalts an ideal concept of Love. Ugly himself, both morally and physically, he makes of Helen a symbol of Beauty, and by his worship of her poses as a devotee of Beauty. He turns cowardice into bravery by setting it in a context of war. As Hecuba comments: 'L'homme en temps de guerre s'appelle le héros. Il peut ne pas en être plus brave, et fuir à toutes jambes. Mais c'est du moins un héros qui détale' (I vi). His poetry does not express his life: it camouflages it with clichés. For him the Symbol is not what it is for Giraudoux—a sign which reveals something of the nature of the world—but a shoddy substitute for lived reality: 'Ainsi le rubis personnifie le sang' (I vi).

This substitution of verbal concepts for lived experience is no less clearly seen in Busiris, the expert on international law. Hector's approach to law is the commonsense one that it exists to protect the innocent. But like any other abstraction it can become an end in itself, entirely divorced from reality. Busiris is devoted to the logic of law, and is totally indifferent to its effects upon people. He is enough of an artist to be able to derive from the same abstract concepts totally opposing conclusions, as the occasion may demand. And he too is thoroughly corrupt. Uninterested in people, he is profoundly interested in himself. The moment he realizes that his ingenious reasonings will land him in gaol, he finds a formula for peace with no difficulty at all.

Once the Ideal is divorced from reality—'[Hélène et Pâris] sont le symbole de l'amour. Ils n'ont plus même à s'aimer' (I vi)—it becomes a refuge for a corrupt humanity. Man's own failings become unimportant when he can identify himself with a great cause. It is easier to fight for Justice than to be just, easier to go on a crusade than to practise religion, easier to be patriotic in war than to serve one's country in peacetime. By proclaiming ourselves the servant of an Ideal, we justify our existence and our own unworthiness becomes a matter of little moment. Priam, a more experienced statesman than Hector and fully aware of the limitations of those he governs, sees this clearly:

> Mon cher fils, regarde seulement cette foule, et tu comprendras ce qu'est Hélène. Elle est une espèce d'absolution. Elle prouve à tous ces vieillards que tu vois là au guet et qui ont mis des cheveux blancs au fronton de la ville, à celui-là qui a volé, à celui-là qui trafiquait des femmes, à celui-là qui manqua sa vie, qu'ils avaient au fond d'eux-mêmes une revendication secrète, qui était la beauté. Si la

beauté avait été près d'eux, aussi près qu'Hélène l'est aujourd'hui, ils n'auraient pas dévalisé leurs amis, ni vendu leurs filles, ni bu leur héritage. Hélène est leur pardon, et leur revanche, et leur avenir (I vi).

Helen is, as she is later to tell Andromache (II viii), a 'vedette'. The essence of stardom is that it enables humanity to escape from the inadequacy of its own existence into a superior dream-world, to identify itself with the supermen it would like to be. The hysteria of the old men of Troy is related to that which, in our own time, has gripped thousands of screaming and swooning teenagers at the merest glimpse of the Beatles; but what in the young may be an outlet for the expression of emotions not yet harnessed to the real business of living becomes, in the old, a sign of barren and ridiculous futility. And it can be extremely dangerous. At the time Giraudoux was writing, in Nazi Germany, vast assemblies of apparently normal adults were working themselves into frenzies, to the hypnotic, repeated chant of 'Sieg Heil', as they awaited the appearance of their dream image Adolf Hitler, who, with his message of hate, had united them in the abstraction of 'Ein Volk, ein Reich, ein Führer'. The puniest of the followers of Hitler felt himself a superman, just as the worshippers of Helen, scampering up and down the staircases of Troy, believe they have recovered their virility and youth. It is a grotesque spectacle, but one which can recur anywhere, in any age, so long as men feel the need to escape from their own inadequacies.

7. *Helen*

Of all the characters which Giraudoux inherited from the story of Troy, Helen was the most enigmatic. She was a daughter of Leda by Jupiter, who, for this amorous adventure, assumed the form of a swan: and Giraudoux's Helen recalls that she was 'née d'un oiseau' (II viii). She alone of the main personalities involved in the struggle for Troy survived the siege unharmed and resumed her life exactly as it had been before the elopement: for her beauty was such that Menelaus took her back again as if nothing had happened in the meantime. And she has survived in the imagination of mankind as the most beautiful of women. As Mr. John Pollard writes in his *Helen of Troy* (Robert Hale, London, 1965):

> It would be wrong to suppose that it was simply and solely sheer sex appeal that men found so irresistible through the ages. It naturally played its part, though it was immeasurably enhanced by the daemonic element latent in Homer's statement that she was 'frighteningly like the immortal goddesses to look upon', coupled with that aura of 'indefinable sadness', to quote Sir Maurice Bowra, 'which goes with great beauty'.

The Helen of *La guerre de Troie n'aura pas lieu* reflects all these qualities, and yet is a strikingly original and giralducian character. His bringing to life of this mythological figure who is at one and the same time both human and superhuman is certainly one of the dramatist's most remarkable achievements. Contrary to the general tendency of modern adaptors of classical myth, who find the supernatural something of an encumbrance, Giraudoux has made more specific the magical powers at which the ancients merely hinted, and has transferred to her the gift of clairvoyance which traditionally belonged to Cassandra.

We see her though the eyes of others long before she actually appears, and the picture we are given is far from flattering. To be the idol of the doting old men of Troy, the inspiration of Demokos' rantings, is bad enough. But scarcely more flattering are Hector's comments—'Je vois deux fesses charmantes' (I vi)—or the jibes of the womenfolk who, here as in Homer, not unnaturally resent her presence among them. When she finally does appear, at the climax of the first act, our impressions do not exactly belie what we have been led to expect. She is beautiful, certainly, but apparently stupid. She repeats like an automaton the phrases Paris has taught her, quite without understanding. At the best, it seems, she is a 'dumb blonde', and perhaps merely a high-class, mentally-retarded prostitute.

Subsequently, we begin to modify this view. What we took for stupidity possibly deserves the name, but it is not a purely negative quality, This is apparent first in her bearing. She possesses what the other characters lack—tranquillity. We may feel, with Hector, that tranquillity is most inappropriate under the circumstances. But we cannot fail to recognize that her detachment from events gives her a dignity which is about the last quality we should expect from what we have heard of her before her appearance.

If we say of her that she is non-rational, amoral and indifferent to human suffering, then we find that we have defined Beauty in Baudelairean terms. We shall not be surprised that with Helen the concept of Destiny comes back into the play. For it is of this same Beauty that Baudelaire wrote: 'Le destin charmé suit tes jupons comme un chien'. Her mind, even if she does not think, comprehends directly 'la forme accélérée du temps'. She does not reason, or follow a course of action because she feels it to be just. She simply sees pictures. She is in the most literal sense a visionary. Among the commonplace, grey images of her daydreams are some which present themselves in vivid colours, and these represent the pre-ordained future. Unlike Rimbaud's *Illuminations*, they are not the active explorations of a human mind, but the reflections of a mechanistic universe. They have no mystery and evoke no wonder: in fact, they evoke no response at all save the passive acceptance of the fact that this is how things will be. One can understand Hector's indignant protest:

> Vous doutez-vous que votre album de chromos est la dérision du monde? Alors que tous ici nous nous battons, nous nous sacrifions pour fabriquer une heure qui soit à nous, vous êtes là à feuilleter vos gravures prêtes de toute éternité!... (I ix)

To understand Helen we must avoid the pitfall (which critics have not always avoided) of supposing that she refuses to return to Greece and so sacrifices Troy to her selfish ends. Since she no longer loves Paris, she has no particular motive for remaining. Nor, as is sometimes assumed, is her subsequent agreement to return motivated by cowardice in the face of Hector's threat to kill her. A glance at the text will be sufficient to establish that the threat has not been uttered or even hinted at when she gives her consent. Hector's failure to influence her is due simply to the fact that she does not act for herself. Her role is passive, rather like that of a spiritualist medium. 'Je laisse l'univers penser à ma place,' she tells Hector. 'Cela, il le fait mieux que moi' (I viii). No amount of persuasion can alter what she sees, for 'ce n'est pas en manœuvrant des enfants qu'on détermine le destin'. The concept of an immutable Destiny is one which Hector can neither understand nor afford to understand, for it would deprive him of all significant motive for action. In a typically giralducian anachronism, attributing to the Greeks a reputation for philosophical speculation which they were not to acquire until a much later period in their history, he cries:

Hector—Les subtilités et les riens grecs m'échappent.

Hélène—Il ne s'agit pas de subtilités et de riens. Il s'agit au moins de monstres et de pyramides. (I ix)

The phrase is obscure. But if we recall the reference to monsters, in *Amphitryon 38*, as 'ces fragments de chaos qui encombrent le travail de la création', and to pyramids, in *Siegfried et le Limousin*, as the most ambitious architectural expression of human power in the context of civilization, we may recognize what such symbols stood for in Giraudoux's imagination and form a conjecture as to Helen's meaning. What seems to Hector to be a mere splitting of philosophical hairs is in fact concerned with the clash between human ambitions and the primeval forces of the world.

Helen is not merely a mirror of Destiny. She is a positive character who has retained the giralducian quality of 'innocence', the capacity to be herself regardless of all moral considerations. She is not, like the old men who worship her, corrupt and self-interested. She does not change her views to suit her convenience or delude herself about the consequences of what she sees. Nor does she opt out of the human condition. Her impassiveness is a stoic reaction to an awareness of that condition. Andromache's accusation that her lack of feeling springs from ignorance of human suffering could not be wider of the mark, as Helen points out in her extended bird-image:

Hélène— . . . Et mon amie au chardonneret était difforme, et mon amie au bouvreuil était phtisique. Et malgré ces ailes que je prêtais au genre humain, je le voyais ce qu'il est, rampant, malpropre et misérable. Mais jamais je n'ai eu le sentiment qu'il exigeait la pitié.

Andromaque—Parce que vous ne le jugez digne que de mépris.

Hélène—C'est à savoir. Cela peut venir aussi de ce que, tous ces malheureux, je les sens mes égaux, de ce que je les admets, de ce que ma santé, ma beauté et ma gloire je ne les juge pas très supérieures à leur misère. Cela peut être de la fraternité.

Andromaque—Vous blasphémez, Hélène.

Hélène—Les gens ont pitié des autres dans la mesure où ils auraient pitié d'eux-mêmes. Le malheur ou la laideur sont des miroirs qu'ils ne supportent pas. Je n'ai aucune pitié pour moi. Vous verrez, si la guerre éclate. Je supporte la faim, le mal sans souffrir, mieux que vous. Et l'injure. Si vous croyez que je n'entends pas les Troyennes sur mon passage! Et elles me traitent de garce! Et elles disent que le matin j'ai l'œil jaune. C'est faux ou c'est vrai. Mais cela m'est égal, si égal!

Andromaque—Arrêtez-vous, Hélène!

> *Hélène*—Et si vous croyez que mon œil, dans ma collection de chromos
> en couleurs, comme dit votre mari, ne me montre pas parfois une
> Hélène vieillie, avachie, édentée, suçotant accroupie quelque confiture
> dans sa cuisine ! [. . .] Et ce que c'est coloré et sûr et certain ! . . . Cela
> m'est complètement indifférent. (II viii)

Since man can neither escape his lot, nor tolerate a mirror which
shows him as he truly is, Helen fulfils her role by providing an image of
Beauty. She does not share Hector's contempt for the old men of Troy,
for she understands their predicament: she is on the same level as they,
but she possesses a Beauty which they need and which she can give. In a
world which is capable of redemption, there is room for the reformer
and the martyr. In a world governed by a complete fatalism, man must
give himself dignity through his imagination. Hence the importance of
the 'vedette' who gives form and style to his dreams and liberates him
from mediocrity. Helen recognizes the legitimacy of both roles:

> Chère Andromaque, tout cela n'est pas si simple. Je ne passe point
> mes nuits, je l'avoue, à réfléchir sur le sort des humains, mais il m'a
> toujours semblé qu'ils se partageaient en deux sortes. Ceux qui
> sont, si vous voulez, la chair de la vie humaine. Et ceux qui
> en sont l'ordonnance, l'allure. Les premiers ont le rire, les pleurs et
> tout ce que vous voudrez en sécrétions. Les autres ont le geste, la
> tenue, le regard. Si vous les obligez à ne faire qu'une race, cela ne
> va plus aller du tout. L'humanité doit autant à ses vedettes qu'à ses
> martyrs. (II viii)

The world, which is 'déjà si nerveux', has need of the tranquil image
which will enable it to escape from itself, and this is what Helen provides.
It is of her very nature to be without *angst*. However, Helen would not
be a living woman if she were without feeling, and Giraudoux's success
in portraying the character depends to no small extent upon his blending
the occasional hint of emotion with her general impassiveness. She
obviously respects Hector and Andromache more than they respect her.
Although her sexual attraction is as much a part of her role in the world
as is her beauty, she makes no attempt to seduce Hector. Indeed, knowing
that for the rest of humanity she exists only as a projection of their own
desires, she shows appreciation, in her opening dialogue with Hector,
of the fact that he is aware of her as a person:

> *Hector*—Je vous demande si c'est beau, la Grèce sans Hélène?
> *Hélène*—Merci pour Hélène. (I viii)

She departs again from her complete impassivity when Hector presses her to describe the scene of his own death. This she can see as clearly as the other events which are to lead to the ruin of Troy. But she does not want to tell him.

> *Hector*—Le groupe Andromaque-Hector . . . Vous le voyez! Ne niez pas! Comment le voyez-vous? Heureux, vieilli, luisant?
> *Hélène*—Je n'essaye pas de le voir.
> *Hector*—Et le groupe Andromaque pleurant sur le corps d'Hector, il luit?
> *Hélène*—Vous savez . . . Je peux très bien voir luisant, extraordinairement luisant, et qu'il n'arrive rien. Personne n'est infaillible.
> (I ix)

Of course, we do not believe her, neither does Hector; but in her refusal to accept the logic of her own vision, she comes alive as a human being. She respects Hector, and, before the final catastrophe, takes sides with him in his efforts to avert it, even though she knows that they will be to no avail. The impassivity with which she faces her own future, and that of humanity, falters when she contemplates his fate:

> Je sens que je vais crier, si vous continuez ainsi, Hector . . . Je vais crier. (I ix)

A reaction as emotional as this, from the mirror of Destiny, is no small tribute to Hector—and to Helen.

We cannot leave her without considering the children of the play, with whom she stands in a special relationship. She understands them because she and they are on the same level. The lack of adult responsibility, which so infuriates Hector in Helen, is natural and acceptable in the child. The parallel between (I vii) and (II vi), with Helen repeating childlike in the first the words of Paris, and Polyxena, in the second, the words of Andromache, can hardly be fortuitous. Both Helen and Polyxena go through the motions of conforming to the wishes of those who are involved in the purely human crisis, but in neither case is the pretence very long sustained.

In Polyxena, Giraudoux gives a delightful thumbnail sketch of childhood, free from sentimentality. Her child's viewpoint enables Polyxena to ignore totally the moral significance of auntie Helen and uncle Demokos in adult affairs. She does not understand death: it is merely one of the innumerable mysteries of the world she has not yet experienced. She can be imaginative, as when she sees the dead pushing the

Gates of War shut, and sadistic, plunging her doll's head into boiling water. She spontaneously imitates her mother in the family dispute (I vi), and thus aligns herself with the peace party; but her constrained obedience to Andromache is powerless against her adoration of Helen (II vi).

This adoration leads us naturally to her brother Troilus, who is seen only in relationship with Helen. In this self-conscious adolescent we see the dawn of the sexual urge of which the old men of Troy have given a grotesque and impotent parody. If we see the end before the beginning it is because the power of the twin forces which Helen represents, beauty and sex, goes on from generation to generation. Troilus is afraid of her beauty and of its power to awaken forces within himself which he does not yet understand. Helen, of course, knows Troilus better than he knows himself. Sexual attraction is independent of those qualities which give the individual person significance, and Helen transfers her affections easily from the elder to the younger brother. Troilus' confused resistance, at the beginning of Act II, leads inevitably to his complete conquest at the end. Human lives and values will be destroyed with the fall of Troy, and Troilus himself will perish in the fighting; but as the Gates of War open before the final curtain to reveal him in Helen's arms, we know that the power of sex and beauty which has brought about this destruction will continue into the future as one of the instruments of destiny, stronger than commonsense, stronger even than the urge for survival.

8. Ulysses

As is only to be expected, the ambassador sent by the Greeks to negotiate the return of Helen is regarded with deep suspicion in Troy. He brings with him the reputation for cunning which is still associated with his name, and this is scarcely reassuring to those who, like Hector, want peace: while he is the natural target for the xenophobic hatred of those who, like Demokos, want war. He himself arrives in Troy with an open mind. He thinks that war is likely, but he does not want it.

To appreciate his position, we must take into account his mythological background. Whether or not Ulysses was one of Helen's suitors is an obscure point—he was probably not, since his own choice was Penelope —but it was he who, with the object of avoiding a resort to violence among the competitors for the hand of this most eligible of Greek women, proposed the pact by which all who sought her in marriage swore to come to the aid of her husband, once he was chosen, should any attempt be made to interfere with the choice. Ulysses himself took the same oath. But when the time came, he was reluctant to keep it. He was happily married and a son, Telemachus, had just been born; and further, it had been prophesied that if he left for Troy he would be away from home for twenty years. His attempt to avoid the call-up was unsuccessful, but there can be no doubt that, when he arrived on the diplomatic visit which is the subject of Giraudoux's play, he wanted a peaceful settlement.

It was in any case in Ulysses' nature to prefer diplomacy to violence. Not that he was a pacifist or an idealist in the sense in which the word is used in common parlance. He was, in the subsequent war, to gain a reputation as one of the bravest of the Greek warriors. And he could be unscrupulous and quite ruthless. According to some accounts, it was he who ordered that Hector's son should be thrown from the battlements during the sack of Troy in order to ensure with the extinction of the royal family that the city should never rise again. If peace was possible, he preferred peace: but once armed conflict became a fact, he accepted its demands and carried them to their logical conclusion without hesitation. The Trojan Horse, a stratagem for which it seems he was responsible, may have become the very symbol of treachery, but it was the means by which the war was won after ten years of indecisive hand-to-hand fighting. Ulysses has had over the ages what we may describe as a bad press, largely because the world is afraid of his particular kind of intelligence, though it is ready enough to make use of it when it gets the chance. He has suffered, in fact, the same fate as Machiavelli, that other political realist whose name gave us, in English, 'Old Nick' as a sobriquet for the Devil.

But there is another side to Ulysses' character. He inspired in his wife Penelope a devotion which has made her proverbial as the faithful spouse, weaving and unpicking her tapestry year after year to keep at bay the importunate suitors who would replace him. We have commented on the fact that, in the context of its time, the love of Hector and Andromache was exceptional. We may say the same of Ulysses.

D

He was a family man, who loved and was loved. During the ten years of wanderings after the sack of Troy which are the subject of the *Odyssey*, he remained faithful to Penelope, save when ensnared by magical charms; and his sole concern was to return to his wife, his child and his homeland. When, after his twenty years' absence, he returned to Ithaca a destitute beggar, only his dog, old and decrepit, recognized him; and the animal, rising to greet him, died of joy.

This complexity in Ulysses is perfectly grasped by Giraudoux. When he agrees to work with Hector to divert the course of Destiny, the young and generous Trojan leader attributes his decision to nobility of heart. But it is not so simple as that.

> *Ulysse*—Vous savez ce qui me décide à partir, Hector . . .
> *Hector*—Je le sais. La noblesse.
> *Ulysse*—Pas précisément. . . . Andromaque a le même battement de cils que Pénélope. (II xiii)

The stress on chance, with its implication of cynicism, is deliberate. But we should misunderstand his reply entirely if we were to overlook the fact that he loved Penelope. A mere transient resemblance enables him to put himself in Hector's position, and to abandon (though not without misgivings) his policy of realism. As Professor Stanford, who has studied the varying fortunes of Ulysses through the literatures of Europe, remarks in *The Ulysses Theme* (Blackwell, Oxford, 1954): 'The phrase, characteristic of his almost frivolous refusal to accept pretentious generalizations in this play, suggests both ironical self-depreciation and also reminds us for an instant of the gentler aspect of the Odyssean hero.' We may well, indeed, quote further from Professor Stanford's assessment of Giraudoux's Ulysses:

> The impact of his portrait is fresh and strong. He appears first as an ambassador among a group of leading Trojans. His manner is forthright, brusque, but not disagreeable, more reminiscent of the scenes with Cressida and Hector in Shakespeare's play than of anything in Euripides, Seneca or Racine. A salty Homeric humour and an unusual candour of phrase make it clear that this is neither the discreet negotiator nor the callous power-politician. [. . .] Giraudoux's Ulysses is a brilliant sketch, combining a Racinian lucidity of phrase and thought with a Homeric and Shakespearian sympathy for Ulysses's essential Greekness. Like all the greater conceptions of Ulysses, this figure succeeds in personifying apparently hostile qualities. He is both fatalistic and energetic, realistic and compassionate, logical and imaginative,

flippant and serious. . . . One recognizes, despite Giraudoux's twentieth-century ethics and idiom, the innate honesty and tolerance of the Homeric hero. [. . .] As in the *Iliad* and in *Troilus and Cressida* the Ulysses of *La guerre de Troie n'aura pas lieu* stands for the civilized mind in a world of undisciplined passion. This is his highest function as a *politique*.

Within a few minutes of his arrival in Troy, Ulysses is aware that he can have war if he wants it. For the situation provoked in (II xii) is far more dangerous than the antics of Demokos earlier in the play. Then it was only the impotent old who were clamouring for war: the young were tired of it, and desired only to return to their homes. But in the face of Hector's well-intentioned lying about the love-life of Paris and Helen, Ulysses' skilful jibes at the virility of the Trojans succeed immediately in uniting young and old in indignant fury. The crisis is only averted by the direct intervention of the gods. Their warning that, unless man can reconcile the irreconcilable, war will follow, is hardly helpful in itself, but it does at least have the effect of taking the decision out of the hands of the angry mob and putting it in those of the two leaders, who thus meet for the final and crucial debate on the issue of peace and war.

What follows is not, in the first place, a rational discussion. The dialogue opens with a weighing in the balance of contrasting images. The two protagonists establish their contrasting visions of the world: the one that of the young man who offers the qualities which would be appropriate in a world in which human values prevailed, the other the experience of a man who has learnt that they do not.

> *Hector*—Je pèse un homme jeune, une femme jeune, un enfant à naître. Je pèse la joie de vivre, la confiance de vivre, l'élan vers ce qui est juste et naturel.
> *Ulysse*—Je pèse l'homme adulte, la femme de trente ans, le fils que je mesure chaque mois avec des encoches, contre le chambranle du palais. [. . .] Je pèse la volupté de vivre et la méfiance de la vie.
> *Hector*—Je pèse la chasse, le courage, la fidélité, l'amour.
> *Ulysse*—Je pèse la circonspection devant les dieux, les hommes et les choses. (I xiii)

The imagery is then transferred to the landscape. Hector evokes the oaks and oxen of his native land, symbols of the strength in which he trusts as well as of his love of the Troad. Ulysses answers with the olive tree, characteristic of Greece and the basis of her economic wealth. Here, one suspects, there may be an allusion to his 'circonspection devant les dieux'—a characteristic of the Homeric Ulysses—for the olive tree was given to Greece by Pallas Athena. Pallas was Ulysses' personal protector and a prime mover in the Trojan War: it was her implacable anger against Paris, who spurned her in favour of Aphrodite when called on to award the golden apple to the fairest of the goddesses, which led to the destruction of Troy. Be that as it may, the allusion is more certain when we pass to bird-images.

> *Hector*—Je pèse le faucon, je regarde le soleil en face.
> *Ulysse*—Je pèse la chouette.

Hector's image is a development of his reference to hunting: the qualities of youthful energy, courage and love of life are vividly expressed. Ulysses answers Hector's allusion to the sun with the bird of night, the owl, traditional symbol of wisdom but with sinister connotations. The owl was the emblem of Pallas Athena, and frequently appears in representations of her.

> *Hector*—Je pèse tout un peuple de paysans débonnaires, d'artisans laborieux, de milliers de charrues, de métiers à tisser, de forges et d'enclumes. [. . .]
> *Ulysse*—Je pèse ce que pèse cet air incorruptible et impitoyable sur la côte et sur l'archipel.

Hector's appeal is similar to that of Andromache when, in the opening scene of the play, she called the industriousness of the fisherfolk around the walls of Troy to witness to the necessity of peace. His image is one of great physical weight, which, in the 'pesée', should surely incline the balance in his direction. But Ulysses places in the scales the pure weightless air, symbol of the infinite and the eternal, and the domain of the gods; and an element which was particularly associated with Pallas. It is in his direction that the balance tilts.

This conflict of images is a most striking example of Giraudoux's exploratory use of symbols. Although one may suggest certain rational implications in the dialogue, its appeal is essentially to the imagination. One image calls up another, as in poetry rime calls up rime, or, in music, phrase answers phrase: and from the contrast there emerges a vivid picture of the 'essence' of Hector and Ulysses. The use of this imaged style enables the play to move imperceptibly at this point from the world of essences to that of the twentieth century. From now on Ulysses dominates the conversation, and although he is still ostensibly speaking of Greece and Troy, his allusions are limited to no particular epoch and are applicable to history in general and often, more especially, to relations between France and Germany in Giraudoux's own time. Thus the reference to the leaders of the nations who meet 'sur la terrasse au bord d'un lac' calls to mind peace conferences held in Switzerland in the inter-war years, upon which the peace of the world seemed to depend in 1935. When Ulysses asserts that 'le privilège des grands, c'est de voir les catastrophes d'une terrasse', he is making it clear that these deliberations do not, in fact, control the course of events.

While Hector persists in his belief that war is the result of enmity, Ulysses suggests that it results from the co-existence of civilizations which are complementary to each other. Giraudoux has in mind a France of humanistic moderation and classical culture, and a Romantic Germany of superhuman aspirations, such as he had contrasted in his first play, *Siegfried*. These nations offered the world two different concepts of civilization. Life would be incomparably richer if we could benefit from both; but, Ulysses suggests, it is an illusion to suppose that they open to us genuine alternatives. To be able to embrace all possibilities would indeed raise man to the level of the gods, but history will see to it that he is not given the chance: for the appearance of two such civilizations leads to 'le déchaînement de cette brutalité et de cette folie humaines qui seules rassurent les dieux. C'est de la petite politique, j'en conviens,' he adds, 'Mais nous sommes chefs d'Etat, nous pouvons bien entre nous deux le dire: c'est couramment celle du Destin.'

War has, he admits, more immediate political and economic causes. The Greeks feel themselves to be 'à l'étroit sur du roc', and German expansionist ambitions, expressed in Hitler's claim to *Lebensraum*, are implied. Germany, with her sick economy, had her eyes on the wealth of other nations. Troy was a rich city, and a temptation to her covetous neighbours. 'Il n'est pas très prudent d'avoir des dieux et des légumes trop dorés.' This at least is a point that Hector can understand.

Whatever may be Ulysses' personal view, the Greeks as a people think they have everything to gain from war. Ambition, xenophobia and covetousness always exist, but for this psychological atmosphere to precipitate a war a certain combination of circumstances is required. The question in Ulysses' mind is whether these circumstances exist. And now, having seen the situation for himself, he thinks that they do.

Troy is ripe for plucking. She has reached the final stage of her civilization.

Ce n'est pas par des crimes qu'un peuple se met en situation fausse avec son destin, mais par des fautes. Son armée est forte, sa caisse abondante, ses poètes en plein fonctionnement. Mais un jour, on ne sait pourquoi, du fait que ses citoyens coupent méchamment les arbres, que son prince enlève vilainement une femme, que ses enfants adoptent une mauvaise turbulence, il est perdu. Les nations, comme les hommes, meurent d'imperceptibles impolitesses. C'est à leur façon d'éternuer ou d'éculer leurs talons que se reconnaissent les peuples condamnés. . . . Vous avez sans doute mal enlevé Hélène.

We have already seen that the first circumstance leading to a state of war is the co-existence of two civilizations, each offering a different future to humanity. The second condition is that the equilibrium between them shall be upset by one of them going into a state of decline. Ulysses is not an abstract thinker: he does not speculate on general causes, but, as a diplomat, observes facts. The facts in themselves appear trivial enough to give a certain tone of frivolity and cynicism to what he says. But they represent a gradual and growing casualness among ordinary people. Ulysses' reference to the barbaric and indiscriminate felling of trees takes on a new sense if we recall his author's lasting concern for the preservation of the French countryside and the beauty of Paris and provincial towns. A year almost to the day before the première of *La guerre de Troie n'aura pas lieu* he had broadcast to the French people:

Combien de vous n'ont été atterrés à voir, du soir au matin, un paysage mutilé, un monument détruit ou masqué par des constructions lamentables, une richesse du passé, une sauvegarde du futur saccagé, non pas par la mauvaise volonté, mais par la distraction ou l'ignorance des municipalités mal averties. On y détruisait tout un manoir pour avoir une seule cheminée, on gâchait tout un site pour une seule usine, tout comme les chasseurs africains sacrifient l'énorme masse d'un éléphant pour avoir ses défenses. Cette méthode amène la disparition des éléphants en Afrique, et elle risque de compromettre non seulement le visage même de notre pays, mais sa santé et sa dignité. (*Avant-scène*, 21 November 1934)

Ulysses sees the wilful destruction or neglect of natural beauties, the abandonment of common refinements of civilized living (as in the reference to sneezing), and hooliganism among young people as indications that a society is losing its self-respect. His claim that a flourishing civilization is marked by good manners rather than good morals is realistic, not cynical. The Italy or England of the Renaissance, the France of Louis XIV, Spain at the height of her power, were at least as corrupt and as socially unjust as other societies: but they excelled in that they conducted their affairs with style. A civilization, Ulysses suggests, declines not through evil-doing but through carelessness: the qualities for which it stands no longer have any meaning for ordinary people.

In a lecture given in 1934, Giraudoux had observed this state of affairs in the France of his own time:

Le nom de la nation contient pour votre imagination toutes ses richesses, sa particularité, son rôle prédestiné dans le théâtre des nations, et il n'est pas un de ces noms qui ne soit pas un programme. Mais le nom du national n'est pas par rapport à ce nom de la nation ce qu'est, par exemple, le mot abeille par rapport au mot ruche. . . . Le mot France évoque, pour celui qui n'est jamais venu en France, la courtoisie, les relations parfaites entre les individus; la France est la maîtresse de cérémonie du monde. Le mot Français évoque un peu trop souvent, au contraire, pour le visiteur étranger, l'individu grincheux, les disputes dans les rues, le chauffeur impoli, les conducteurs de tramway mal élevés. Le mot France évoque l'idée d'une nation politique constante, d'une stabilité morale inattaquable; le mot Français l'idée d'une variation continuelle et d'une incertitude. . . (*La Française et la France*)

The doomed civilization, says Ulysses, may be extremely prosperous. And one may add, in comment, that if one seeks economic causes for the decline of Rome or Spain or Portugal, once masters of sizeable areas of the world, one is more likely to find them in a surfeit of wealth than a lack. And that civilization, as expressed by an élite of artists and writers, may be brilliant, but it is consuming the capital of the past and not replacing it. Indeed, a culture may live on, as did that of classical Greece, long after the people who produced it have disintegrated into insignificance. In this field, too, Giraudoux viewed the France of his time with misgiving, as we see from his *Introduction à la Charte d'Athènes:*

Il est à craindre que la mission et la conscience nationales ne soient l'apanage exclusif d'une cohorte de plus en plus raréfiée au centre d'un pays que gagnent la banalité et l'insensibilité universelles. Il est à craindre que le soin de conserver sa raison à la nation ne soit un jour réservé à une caste, à une oligarchie, que le génie du pays ne soit plus la fonction du pays dans son ensemble et dans sa masse, n'en soit

plus la sève, mais l'acte cérébral d'une intelligence de plus en plus
isolée. . . .

When a civilization is exhausted, it ceases to adapt itself to its age and
it loses its sense of vocation. It no longer has a contribution to make to the
world. This is the situation which Ulysses observes in Troy. The abduction of Helen was not a heroic gesture, an expression of a positive admira-
tion for Love and Beauty. The old men of Troy adore Helen because
they are too impotent to love or produce beauty themselves. Her coming
precipitates the decline of Troy as surely as did the influx of gold
from South America that of Spain and Portugal.

Ulysses has now presented two stages in the progress towards war—
war seen in twentieth-century terms as a universal holocaust rather
than as the conflict between cities and princelings of primitive times.
The first stage was the existence of two alternative ways of life—France
and Germany, Giraudoux would have said in his own time, but we
today would think in terms of communism and capitalism, or totalitar-
ianism and individualistic democracy. The second is that one of these
should decline—not in terms of morality, for on that basis there may be
very little to choose between them, but in terms of the degree of relevance which their basic principles, their *raison d'être*, have to the life of
the ordinary man in the street. This produces a state of potential war.
But between potential war and the actual horror of its outbreak there
is all the difference in the world. And that difference, Ulysses goes on to
say, depends on factors which border on pure chance, and can only be
estimated empirically.

Vous vous êtes trompés sur Hélène, Pâris et vous. Depuis quinze
ans je la connais, je l'observe. Il n'y a aucun doute. Elle est une des
rares créatures que le destin met en circulation sur la terre pour son
usage personnel. Elles n'ont l'air de rien. Elles sont parfois une bour-
gade, presque un village, une petite reine, presque une petite fille,
mais si vous les touchez, prenez garde! C'est là la difficulté de la vie,
de distinguer, entre les êtres et les objets, celui qui est l'otage du
destin. Vous ne l'avez pas distingué.

Let us consider one example which Giraudoux may have had in mind.
The Archduke Francis Ferdinand of Austria was not, apparently, a figure
of major political importance. Nor was the province of Serbia, nor the
little town of Sarajevo. When, in 1914, a terrorist organization known
as the Black Hand assassinated him there, it was concerned solely with

a minor adjustment of boundaries in southern Europe. But his death was the immediate cause of the First World War, and changed irrevocably the whole history of mankind. However many causes historians and economists and others whose task it is to introduce a semblance of rationality into the human story may bring forward, the fact remains that without this event a state of potential war might not have become one of actual war. But once the act was perpetrated, the subsequent course of events was irreversible.

As Ulysses recognizes, such spectacular demonstrations of the role of chance in human affairs are not common. Hostages of destiny are rare: it is Troy's misfortune that Helen is one of them. They are people or things the disturbance of which produces consequences totally out of proportion to anything which might be anticipated. They turn the course of history in new directions.

Ulysses' view of destiny is not cosmic, like that of Cassandra. Nor, like that of Helen, is it fatalistic. Destiny is, for him, a force over which man has little control, but it is the product of political and economic circumstances. As he says to Hector:

> Ne m'en veuillez pas d'interpréter le sort. J'ai voulu seulement lire dans ces grandes lignes que sont, sur l'univers, les voies des caravanes, les chemins des navires, la trace des grues volantes et des races.

But it would be unrealistic not to recognize that, when one interprets Ulysses' words in terms of Giraudoux's sociological thinking, one is paraphrasing them and filling in their background rather than reproducing the effect they have in the theatre. For, as the above quotation abundantly illustrates, his approach to history is not so much analytical as a form of divination. He sees life as a gamble. Certainly there are rules to the game, and it is essential to know them; but living is very much like playing a game of poker. One can never be quite sure what cards Destiny holds in her hand. Ulysses does not lecture Hector on politics or economics. He gives intuitive impressions. But at least his concept of Destiny allows him the freedom to play his hand, even when he knows that the odds are against him. This is precisely what he does when he throws in his lot with Hector. But before Ulysses completes his long walk to where the Greek ships are drawn up on the beach, Demokos dies, Oiax dies, and war is declared.

9. Conclusion

Giraudoux might never have written for the theatre had it not been for the influence of Louis Jouvet, one of the great actor-managers of the French theatre in the first half of the twentieth century. The degree of understanding which existed between these two men was remarkable. Giraudoux had in fact already written at least a part of *Siegfried*—a dramatic adaptation of one of his novels—before he was introduced to Jouvet, and the circumstances which awakened his interest in this medium at a comparatively late stage in his literary career remain obscure; but it was certainly Jouvet who made him into a professional man of the theatre and taught him to translate his highly individual style and vision into a form which had an immediate impact on the audiences of the time. Apart from *Pour Lucrèce*, which M. Jean-Louis Barrault produced after both men were dead, all Giraudoux's plays were given their final form by Louis Jouvet, and every role was written by Giraudoux with a particular actor or actress of his troupe in mind. Jouvet himself was an artist of great integrity and intelligence. He could scarcely have realized, when he staged *Siegfried*, that he was taking a first decisive step which would change the whole direction of the modern French theatre. But that is what happened. With Giraudoux, the theatre became one of the most important media of modern French literature, exploring ideas in a manner which was truly dramatic, appealing to the imagination as well as to the mind and the emotions, and restoring to language the pre-eminence which it had enjoyed in all the great periods of the history of the stage.

So close was the co-operation between Giraudoux and Jouvet's troupe that he once declared, in a lecture which was subsequently published in *Littérature*, that 'il n'y a pas d'auteur au théâtre': a play should be considered as an anonymous work like the great cathedrals, since it is the joint product of so many talents.

But this view must be considered in the light of another, apparently contradictory to it, which was held equally firmly by both Giraudoux and Jouvet. This was that theatre is a form of literature and the sole function of producer and actors is to interpret the text. In *l'Impromptu de Paris* Giraudoux puts into Jouvet's mouth the definition of the actor as 'la statue à peine animée de la parole'. This concept of acting contributes to the static quality we notice in *La guerre de Troie n'aura pas lieu*—the characters talk and rarely actually do anything, and stage directions are reduced to the minimum—and derives from Jouvet's own personal style of acting as much as from Giraudoux's models in the Greek and French classical theatre.

The two views are not really contradictory. Of all arts acting is one of the most ephemeral: tastes change, and if we today could see some of the greatest actors of the past in their greatest roles, we should probably find them ludicrous. A producer of *La guerre de Troie n'aura pas lieu* in our own time would be unlikely to take Jouvet as his model. The task of the actor is to interpret for his own age a text intended for all ages. If he fails, the text remains inaccessible to his audience. Our own preoccupations are not identical with those of the pre-war generation and this fact will modify, for us, the 'meaning' of the author's text. The actor is a vital link in making this transition possible.

Certain features must of course be constant in any production. Hector and Andromache must engage our sympathies by their youthful idealism. Demokos must be ridiculous. Ulysses must contrast with Hector by reason of his greater maturity, his sophistication, his touch of cynicism. But his essentially civilized humanity, his capacity for generosity, must colour our response to his otherwise somewhat sinister role. If our reaction to him is as naïve as that of Andromache—'cet homme est effroyable'—then the play becomes unbalanced. Helen must possess a quality of mystery and dignity which will prevent us from regarding her, as Hector does, simply as a nuisance to be got rid of. Unless this is achieved, the play becomes a sham battle. Among the old men of Troy, King Priam must have a regal bearing, the vestiges of a past authority to make us aware that what he has to say is based on long experience of governing men. Cassandra must not merely discourse on metaphysical abstractions: she must make us feel her anguish and involvement, and the insuperable barrier of knowledge which separates her from the innocent hopes of Andromache.

But there are innumerable nuances of tone and gesture and atmosphere which will vary from production to production, even from performance to performance. The dramatist does not present a one-sided view, forcing our sympathies in one direction only. The temptation to divide the characters into 'goodies' and 'baddies', to assume that Giraudoux offers us Hector as a model to be imitated and all his opponents as objects of hate, must be recognized for what it is—an irrelevant survival of the doubtless instinctive human desire that every story shall have a moral. Giraudoux himself never professed to know the 'meaning' of his plays in this sense. What he does is to put into the producer's hands a variety of forces, some favourable and others inimical to our accepted view of human interests, which the producer turns loose to do battle on his stage. What matters, in dramatic terms, is not whether the Trojan War will take place, but the sensitivity of our own response to the complex of forces which produce it.

It is therefore quite useless, and indeed misleading, to look to *La guerre de Troie n'aura pas lieu* for a single message. It is a living dramatic performance, and no simple theory lies behind it. It enables us to view factors relevant to the human condition in a perspective which the humdrum routine of daily living does not permit. It gives us, as it were, a sort of divine vision. When Ulysses declares: 'Le privilège des grands, c'est de voir les catastrophes d'une terrasse', he is incidentally giving quite a good definition of the audience in the theatre.

It may be suggested that, in the place of a clear 'meaning', *La guerre de Troie n'aura pas lieu* has three characteristics which appeal to our sensibility and thus contribute not merely to our knowledge but to the wisdom of our approach to living.

In the first place Hector dominates the play, if not the events, and as a result it is suffused from beginning to end with his generosity, his courage, his youthfulness and his love of life. Giraudoux has seen to it that the most memorable and moving speech in the whole text is his address to the dead, which is, paradoxically but deliberately, a hymn to life. Even if, in political terms, Hector may be wrong in his assessment of the situation, no one in the theatre will have any doubt that he is right to be wrong. It is his stand, and not that of his opponents, which is the expression of man's hopes.

Secondly, the richness and vividness of the language makes the play a significant and moving aesthetic experience. Whereas subsequent writers of the theatre of the absurd have deliberately cultivated the disintegration of language, Giraudoux does the opposite. His play is a work of art, not an indignant protest against the meaninglessness of the universe. On an aesthetic level he makes some sense of life, and he would claim that this imaginative comprehension is a good deal more valid than intellectual pessimism. Thirdly, the element of comedy in his treatment of

the theme is so pronounced as to prevent us from adopting a purely pessimistic response, even though our rational interpretation of the ideas
may lead us in that direction. It is an antidote to the temptation to
romanticize and wallow in self-pity. To speak of the universe as absurd
is, after all, to make a statement not about the universe but about the
limitations of the human intellect, in which case it is unwise to take
our predicament too seriously, for we do not really understand it or
recognize it for what it is.

We have seen that André Gide disliked the importance which Giraudoux gives to chance in the action of his play, and held that this invali-
dated it both aesthetically and morally. Chance presents a particular
difficulty for writers. We are all aware of the important part it plays
in our lives, but the reader does not readily accept it in the plot of a
story. But since Gide wrote, the concept of the 'absurd universe' has
become a literary commonplace, and we can appreciate more easily
than he the importance of this theme in Giraudoux. Gide belonged to a
literary tradition which was concerned almost exclusively with psychological motivation and the morality of human relationships in society.
The physical world, in that tradition, was no more than a backcloth
which as often as not could be taken for granted, or, if consciously used,
served only to set off human emotion and behaviour. Our own view
has been changed by circumstances. For Giraudoux, man was a stranger
on an alien planet. Although in our own time this sense of alienation
has been expressed in existentialist philosophies, it is in no sense new:
on the contrary it is as old as thinking man, even though it has not until
recently formed the mainstream of French literature. The earliest myths
are man's first known attempts to give sense to his world. And in the
sophisticated society of eighteenth-century France Voltaire gave the
absurdity of the human condition its most trenchant expression in
Candide. Thus, although Giraudoux's preoccupations are a reflection
of those of the modern world, we should not associate him too exclusively
with what, in the years following his death, we have come to know as
'the theatre of the absurd'. Both Giraudoux and, after him, Camus
stand apart from most 'absurdist' trends in modern literature by reason
of a love of life and a respect for the human condition which they
inherit from classical Greece.

But Gide's criticism of *La guerre de Troie n'aura pas lieu* may still have a
certain validity which the student of Giraudoux must judge for himself.
He is by no means the only critic to consider that Giraudoux's treatment

of his theme is too whimsical to reflect its inherent seriousness. Giraudoux, they would object, lacks indignation and anguish, and his humour and irony take the sting out of his presentation of the human tragedy. And the uncertainty of intellectual response which this may encourage is aggravated, they would hold, by the obscurity of his style.

When, for instance, Ulysses tells us that the collapse of a civilization is shown by the way in which people sneeze or chop down their trees, the disproportion between these events is such that, unless we are able to interpret them in the light of Giraudoux's thought as a whole, the statement may strike us as wilfully and pointlessly paradoxical. Exactly the same disproportion is present when William Blake, for instance, tells us that

> A dog starved at his Master's Gate
> Predicts the ruin of the State

but our reaction is likely to be different because the moral link implied is simple and obvious. Giraudoux's expression, on the other hand, leaves a great deal of room for the imagination to work. Whether it would be possible to interweave themes as intellectually irreconcilable as those which Giraudoux handles in a language which appeals directly to the intellect is a matter for conjecture. Whether one likes it or not, Giraudoux's thought expressed itself spontaneously in images: he did not first think of an idea and then find a suitable image to express it. The result of his use of language is an imaginative experience which one likes or dislikes, but is any in case essential to Giraudoux's art.

Out of a predicament which, viewed in strictly realistic terms, represents a stupid waste of human potential, he creates a play which intensifies our awareness of human dignity. This play is not optimistic, but neither, as a dramatic experience, is it pessimistic. It recognizes the limits of the human condition and gives them significance. We may apply to his art the words which he himself, in *La Française et la France*, applies to French civilization:

> . . . Tout en réservant tous les droits d'un être supérieur ou d'un chaos fondemental, de la religion ou de la philosophie, elle a [. . .] trouvé le rapport exact de l'homme par rapport à la planète, de l'homme par rapport à la longueur de sa vie, par rapport aux joies et souffrances qu'il peut éprouver dans ce bas monde. Elle a ménagé le maximum de liberté morale et physique à ce prisonnier sur le globe.

Bibliographical Note

La guerre de Troie n'aura pas lieu, which was first performed at the
Théâtre de l'Athénée, Paris, on 21 November 1935, with Louis Jouvet as
Hector is published—as are all Giraudoux's works—by Grasset (Paris).
It is also included, together with some variant readings of the text, in the
Théatre complet de Jean Giraudoux, published by Ides et Calendes (Neuf-
chatel, 1943–48). It has been translated into English by Mr. Christopher
Fry under the title of *Tiger at the Gates* (Methuen, 1955). This is an
excellent version for the theatre, but should not be regarded as in any
way a substitute for the French text: for instance, the translation of
'la forme accélérée du temps' as 'the relentless logic of each day we live',
and the omission of Helen's 'vedette' speech, obviously deprive the
play of important elements of the complex of ideas which it represents,
and no translation can adequately reflect Giraudoux's style.

For the student, the most useful edition is that published by Grasset
in the series Livres de Poche Université (Paris, 1964) with notes and
commentary by M. Etienne Frois which also serve to place the play in the
context of Giraudoux's work as a whole. The student may consult with
equal profit the Introduction and notes by M. Maurice Mercier in the
series Classiques Larousse (Librairie Larousse, Paris, 1959): the text of
this edition is somewhat abbreviated. The edition of the play prepared
by Dr. H. J. G. Godin for the series *Textes Français Classiques et Modernes*
(University of London Press, 1958) throws valuable light on many aspects
of the text, but is a more individualistic interpretation which should be
studied in association with those mentioned above. The text which
appears in Volume II of Clouard & Leggewie's *Anthologie de la littérature
française* (New York, 1960) is annotated on a very elementary level.

It is impossible to refer here to the abundant literature on Giraudoux.
Donald Inskip, in his *Jean Giraudoux, the Making of a Dramatist* (Oxford
University Press, London, 1958), gives a good straightforward account
of the plays and their theatrical background: Robert Cohen, in his
Giraudoux: Three Faces of Destiny (University of Chicago Press, Chicago
and London, 1968), offers a more recent and theoretical analysis of the
work. The *Tulane Drama Review*, Volume III (Tulane University, New

Orleans 18, Louisiana) contains a number of contributions on Giraudoux, including those by Robert Peacock and Eugene Falk which deal specifically with *La guerre de Troie n'aura pas lieu*. Mr. Paul A. Mankin also deals with the play in his penetrating and highly recommended study of an important aspect of Giraudoux's vision: *Precious Irony* (Mouton, The Hague and Paris, 1971). Giraudoux's use of myth in the theatre is compared with that of his contemporaries in Hugh Dickinson's *Myth on the Modern Stage* (University of Illinois Press, 1969). There are also, of course, sections devoted to Giraudoux in a large number of books on the modern theatre.

A convenient and readable short introduction to Giraudoux's work as a whole, with numerous extracts from both plays and novels, is *Giraudoux par lui-même* by Christian Marker (Editions du Seuil, Paris, 1952). The more advanced student will wish to consult *Esthétique et Morale chez Jean Giraudoux* by René-Marill Albérès (Nizet, Paris, 1962). A sensitive and sympathetic portrait of Giraudoux as a man will be found in two essays by M. Paul Morand published under the title *Jean Giraudoux: Souvenirs de notre jeunesse* (La Palatine, Geneva, 1948).